Exposing the Two Big Lies of the Gun Control Movement

Replacing Gun Control With Violence Control

By James Ostrowski

Cazenovia Books
Buffalo, New York
LibertyMovement.org

In honor of my sister Mary Ostrowski,
head of the Family now with Mom gone.
You have always had our backs.

When the Cambrian measures were forming, They
promised perpetual peace.
They swore, if we gave them our weapons, that
the wars of the tribes would cease.
But when we disarmed They sold us and delivered
us bound to our foe,
And the Gods of the Copybook Headings said:
"Stick to the Devil you know."

--Rudyard Kipling

Table of Contents

Acknowledgements

Sam Sanfratello, a business consultant from New York who has a degree in statistics from the Rochester Institute of Technology, did a great job crunching the numbers for the Global Violence Index.

I want to thank PorcFest, the leading libertarian event of the year on the planet, for allowing me to speak last year about the subject of this book. That speech opportunity provided the motivation to develop the thesis of the book in detail.

My daughter Anna, B. A. in history from Sarah Lawrence College (studied abroad at Wadham College, Oxford), whose love of books is extraordinary, was the chief editor for the book and missed no error, large or small. My wife Amy and son Will also helped in many ways to prepare the manuscript for publication.

I want to take this opportunity to thank the many people in the last 45 years who provided invaluable assistance or encouragement through my long, often-frustrating slog through the mine fields and the lean years of the Liberty Movement. I can't possibly name them all here but I remember all of you, believe me, including many who have passed on.

Each and every one of you contributed in some way to this book, my best and most important, by providing me with the encouragement, inspiration and very often the shekels to carry on the fight.

As recent events proved once again, the Liberty Movement always buries its undertakers.[1] Excelsior!

James Ostrowski
Buffalo, New York
June 2024

---

[1] Paraphrasing Étienne Gilson's famous aphorism that "philosophy always buries its undertakers."

Preface

What is the biggest problem faced by human beings in the last ten thousand years? Gang violence. Government is the biggest, most powerful gang of them all. Libertarians proposed the solution around 1750: the right to bear arms. It worked! Gang and government violence was reduced and restrained. *Where this right was not enforced,* unrestrained gang and government violence continued unabated.

The gun control movement wants to destroy the right to bear arms and revert to our age-old predicament in which the individual was helpless against the gang or government. As it is one of the most sophisticated propaganda efforts of modern times, it is a serious threat to succeed in this mission.

In this book, the sinister agenda, motives and lies of the gun control movement are exposed, dissected, refuted and replaced by a revolutionary new system for identifying and quantifying all the main sources and causes of violence in this world.

That accomplished, we can then propound, pursue and execute numerous concrete proposals to significantly decrease violence and increase peace and liberty, peace and liberty being the exact same thing!

We *can* replace the failed gun control movement with a violence control movement and build a more peaceful world.

Introduction

This book is the sequel to *The Second Amendment Works!: A Primer on How to Defend Our Most Important Right* (2020). That primer contained a wide-ranging reconstruction and defense of the right to bear arms as primarily aimed at deterring government tyranny. Properly understood, the success of the right could be shown by a massive amount of variegated empirical and historical evidence. The evidence supporting the efficacy of the right to bear arms included:

1. The stability and longevity of the Constitution
2. The frequency of coups in countries with a *low* level of civilian gun ownership
3. Low levels of democide[2] compared to countries with low levels of civilian gun ownership
4. The infrequency of foreign invasion (1812-1815)
5. The efficacy of an armed population in repelling invasion (1812-1815)
6. The rarity of combat deaths in the mainland United States (after 1865)
7. The infrequency of civil war compared to countries with low levels of civilian gun ownership (1861-1865)

---

[2] Government murdering non-combatants.

8.   The infrequency of shooting unarmed protesters

9.   The absence of death camps and rarity of concentration camps

10.   The frequency of collapsed democracies in countries with a low level of civilian gun ownership

11.   Compared to other large, diverse countries, the much higher degree of individual freedom in the United States

12.   People voting with their feet to move to the United States, the country with by far the most guns per capita

13.   Inside the United States, people moving from strict gun control states to constitutional carry states (see Table No. 1)

14.   Refugees to the United States predominantly come from countries with very low levels of civilian gun ownership.

15.   The United States leads the world in foreign investment.[3]

16.   The United States is third in global tourism to France/Spain which are contiguous and closer to nearby wealthy and densely populated countries.

---

[3] "U.S. Remains World's Top Destination for Foreign Direct Investment for 12th Consecutive Year," Dept. Commerce, April 4, 2024.

17.   The United States has had the largest
and most innovative economy on Earth
since the late 19th century.

Table No. 1
Americans Vote With Their Feet
for the Second Amendment

Sources: Wikipedia; Giffords.org.

STATES WITH
LARGEST
IN-MIGRATION
WITH GUN
CONTROL
RANKING

1. Florida (24)
2. Texas (31)
3. North Carolina (22)
4. Arizona (41)
5. South Carolina (28)
6. Tennessee (39)
7. Georgia (33)
8. Idaho (46)
9. Alabama (35)
10. Oklahoma (35)
Average—33.34

STATES WITH
LARGEST
OUT-MIGRATION
WITH GUN
CONTROL
RANKING

1. California (1)
2. New York (5)
3. Illinois (4)
4. Massachusetts (7)
5. New Jersey (2)
6. Louisiana (32)
7. Maryland (8)
8. Michigan (17)
9. Ohio (25)
10. Minnesota (15)
Average—11.6

The leading gun control groups, Everytown for Gun
Safety and Giffords Law Center could hardly say they were

unaware of the *Primer*, as it was cited in a Supreme Court brief in a case where each had filed *amici curiae* briefs in the United States Court of Appeals for the Second Circuit. *Libertarian Party of Erie County v. Andrew Cuomo,* Supreme Court Docket No. 20-1151.[4] (The author represented the plaintiffs.) Yet, no rebuttal was ever forthcoming and, to no one's surprise, these groups continue to press their argument, using misleading statistics. I decided I needed to write a sequel to the *Primer* to refute those fallacious statistical arguments once and for all.

Thus, the goal of this book is to destroy the gun control movement in the United States with two separate metaphorical kill shots corresponding to the two main statistical fallacies discussed in this book.

"Gun control" is of course a euphemism. We could just as easily call it the gun owner control movement, gun grabber movement or the government gun monopoly movement. For the sake of simplicity, let's just call it gun control and the gun control movement. They don't want to control *guns;* they want to use government guns to control *people.*

Even though "gun control" is a euphemism, the gun control movement in recent years has started to move away from the term as it conveys a bit more of the authoritarian nature of their desired policy than the mendacious movement desires. Thus, the gun control movement is moving toward an even more deceptive Orwellian

---

[4] Cited in *New York State Rifle & Pistol Association, Inc. v. Bruen,* 597 U.S. 1 (2022), Note 4, as having been wrongly decided.

euphemism, "gun safety." No thanks. I will stick with the term in common usage for decades.

What precisely is gun control? This question is rarely asked or answered. What exactly is the gun control *movement?* This question is never even asked.

Gun control is the use of actual and threatened government gun violence against peaceful people to violate their natural right to keep and bear arms to protect their natural rights[5] to life, liberty and property. Gun control *is* gun violence, specifically the most pernicious form of gun violence, *government gun violence against peaceful people.* It is the most pernicious and dangerous form because of its *inescapability.* You can run from a mugger. Lock your doors. Install security cameras and sound detectors. With a firearm, you can protect yourself from a robber or burglar or rapist. You can avoid walking in high-crime neighborhoods and you can move to a safer neighborhood. How do you escape *government* gun violence? History has shown that can be accomplished only with great difficulty. SpaceX might help. Progressives,[6] the same people who advocate gun control, have destroyed yet another right propounded by the historical libertarians, *freedom of movement.* In this world, with few exceptions, you need permission of at least *two* governments to travel. Thus, thanks to progressives, to escape government violence, you need the government's

---

[5] A "natural right" is a right that exists independently of whether it is recognized by any particular government.

[6] Those who believe that aggressive government force can improve society. See, J. Ostrowski, *Progressivism: A Primer* (2014). "Leftist" is a different concept in my view and usage.

permission to travel. You need *the perpetrator's* permission to travel.

Government gun violence thus has three important features that make it quite insidious: its *inescapability*, its astronomical *frequency* (see Chapter 2) and its deadly *efficiency* (see Chapter 3). We begin to see here the truly *pernicious* nature of gun control and the gun control movement. Its advocates wish to greatly *increase* the amount of government gun violence in society, and specifically the number of traffic stops, no-knock searches at dawn, arrests, prosecutions, pretrial detentions and post-conviction incarcerations lasting decades, in a society already jam-packed with traffic stops, no-knock searches at dawn, arrests, pretrial detentions lasting years, and post-conviction incarcerations. Since every law carries with it an implied threat to *kill* anyone who resists the law,[7] gun control advocates are in favor of enacting hundreds of additional laws that essentially authorize the government *to kill* any number of peaceful Americans whenever necessary.

Gun control is the advocacy of massive aggressive violence in society! To what end? Precisely to destroy the natural right of self-defense against criminals, mobs and governments, and to once again leave citizens at the mercy of criminals, mobs and governments, as they were throughout the violent history of the human race before the libertarians of the day propounded the right to bear arms circa 1750 and installed it into positive law in the Second Amendment in 1791.

So, we finally know exactly what gun control is: the use of massive government gun violence against peaceful people to destroy their natural

---

[7] NY Penal Law § 35.30.

right of self-defense and leave them forever defenseless against aggression from all sources.

What is the gun control *movement?* Who is pushing this insidious idea, how and why?

If you take a close look at who is funding the gun owner control movement, you quickly find some of the wealthiest people in the country. See Table No. 2. The largest gun control group, Everytown for Gun Safety, is funded by Michael Bloomberg, whose net worth is $96 billion.[8] He has multiple homes (castles) with the most sophisticated security imaginable and is known to be guarded by at least four armed guards when he ventures out in public. Politically, he is a classic progressive authoritarian control freak who stupidly believes there is a government gun solution to almost any human problem.[9] He famously sought to ban large servings of soft drinks when he was Mayor of New York City. This is an ideological pattern with almost no exceptions in the gun control movement. Its leaders, funders, staff and operatives are virtually all *progressives* who favor a much larger government than the one favored by the Founding Fathers who drafted the Second Amendment.

We already know from *The Second Amendment Works* that widespread civilian gun ownership tends to deter the growth of big government. Thus, it is obvious that the gun control movement has an ulterior motive they never acknowledge.

---

[8] *Source:* Forbes.

[9] See, James Ostrowski, *Progressivism: A Primer on the Idea Destroying America* (2014).

It will be much easier to expand government when the population is fully disarmed. Here are just a few recent examples. As the aftermath of the 2021 coup d'etat in Myanmar (Burma) shows, it is difficult for citizens to resist an authoritarian regime without weapons. Indeed, the military junta that runs Myanmar recently enacted a new gun control law precisely to prevent the people from restoring democracy. [10] Also noteworthy are the draconian Covid Lockdown in Australia—police firing rubber bullets at Lockdown protesters[11] after strict gun control was enacted there; the horrendous Lockdown in China—people being welded into their apartments [12] —where civilians have virtually no access to weapons; and the slow destruction of a once-thriving country, Venezuela, after strict gun control was enacted, resulting in protesters being shot dead in the street.[13] As noted in the *Primer,* shooting unarmed protesters is a *feature* of many strict gun control regimes. Is it any surprise that authoritarian regimes *love* gun control? Second Amendment scholar Don B. Kates wrote in 2006: "The international gun control movement enjoys the enthusiastic support of Iran, Zimbabwe, Cambodia and various other nations that have already perpetrated genocides or are good

---

[10]   rfa.org/english/news/myanmar/junta-weapons-law-05182023164647.html

[11] city-journal.org/article/no-liberty-no-problem

[12]   gizmodo.com/china-relaxes-harshest-covid-19-rules-after-protests-1849862755

[13] amnesty.org/en/latest/news/2019/01/venezuela-more-than-a-dozen-people-killed-in-protests/

candidates for doing so in the future."[14] We can add China to the chorus.

A careful analysis of key figures in the gun control movement shows that they are almost exclusively progressive *Democrats* who favor a much larger government. The Democrats have been the party of big government since 1913, flipping roles with the Republicans who had served that role from 1861 onward.[15] Many key gun controllers were also high-level Democratic operatives at one time or another. Theory and experience show that a well-armed civilian population is a deterrent to massive and sudden increases in state power. Little else is such a deterrent since the natural tendency of government is to grow continually until it begins to destroy the society upon which it predates. A good example is the Soviet Union, which was taken over by sociopaths (Bolsheviks) in 1917. This wretched regime was able to maintain power through many brutal decades until the society itself started to collapse and the regime itself suddenly collapsed in 1991.

A well-armed civilian population is one of the few dynamics that militates against excessive government growth. The political class always has to wonder if they carry their plans a bit too far they might engender active resistance. History shows that even strong regimes can fall very quickly when the mysterious elixer of power that sustains them suddenly vanishes. Will the public begin to resist as is their

---

[14] "Genocide, Self Defense and the Right to Bear Arms," 29 *Hamline L. Rev.* 501 (Summer, 2006).

[15] Since 1913, the GOP has served as the pretend opposition party which opposes bigger government in theory but never in actual practice when they achieve power.

right under the Declaration of Independence? Without the means to do so, there is no such deterrent to endless government growth.

I should note that history shows that sometimes civil war is planned out but it can also happen inadvertently, as small incidents escalate into large ones. There is a mutual uncertainty in these matters as both governments and populations never quite know how the other will respond to such incidents and escalations. I submit again that this uncertainty is a good thing as it may serve to restrain and rein in governments that would otherwise grow unrestrained for decades.

We do know that it has been common in history for authoritarian regimes to systematically disarm their populations. "Almost without exception, genocide is preceded by a very careful government program that disarms the future victims of genocide. The historical record is quite clear that genocide is almost never attempted against an armed populace."[16]

Though gun controllers frequently complain about the crime and violence committed with *handguns*, they nevertheless have a strong focus on banning, limiting or licensing *semi-automatic rifles* which they misleadingly call "assault rifles." As technological progress goes, semiautomatics are hardly new or sophisticated weapons. They largely replaced bolt-action rifles which predominated from the late 19th century through the early days of World

---

[16] David B. Kopel et al., Gun Ownership and Human Rights, 9.2 *Brown J. of World Aff.* 9 (2003).

War II.[17] The use of semiautomatic rifles[18] in battle dates to 1911, yet we are led to believe this is some fantastic new weapon.[19]

The gun controllers want to disarm citizens and send them back to the old days of single shot rifles, while the government itself not only uses semiautomatic rifles, "assault rifles," but has full access to machine guns and many other powerful weapons such as drones. A complete ban on semiautomatics means that the public would likely never be able to resist well-armed tyrannical regimes and would be forced to accept proto-totalitarian government. As Orwell wrote, "If you want a picture of the future, imagine a boot stamping on a human face—forever." All successful guerrilla movements in modern times used semiautomatic rifles as one of their primary weapons. Thus, as usual, if you look beneath the disingenuous gun control agenda, you see a hidden and sinister motive. Rifles are implicated in only 2.6 percent of street crime.[20] Yet, gun control advocates' primary focus is disarming law-abiding Americans whose families have very often had long guns for generations for self-defense and hunting and defeating Redcoats at Lexington and Concord.

It doesn't take Sherlock Holmes to figure out what is going on here. People who want government much, much bigger than it is now, want to take away one of the few ways people can restrain the natural tendency of government to

---

[17] https://en.wikipedia.org/wiki/Bolt_action

[18] That reload the next bullet when the previous bullet is fired.

[19] https://en.wikipedia.org/wiki/Semi-automatic_rifle

[20] *Source:* FBI.

grow: a well-armed civilian population. Their focus is not on the kinds of guns most used in crime or, God forbid any of the myriad causes of crime. Rather, their primary focus is taking away from law-abiding Americans the gun most useful for exercising their right to re-assume their sovereignty, their right to alter or abolish the government when they, *in their sole discretion*, decide it has lapsed into tyranny: the semiautomatic ("assault") rifle. To paraphrase the left, when authoritarian regimes tell you who they are, believe them!

WHO FUNDS THE GUN CONTROL MOVEMENT?

Table No. 2

Gun Control Advocate/ Affiliation	Occupation	Net worth	Connections with the Democratic Party
Michael Bloomberg/ EveryTown	CEO, Bloomberg LP	$96 billion	Huge donor and sometime candidate
Ronald Conway/ Giffords	Venture Capitalist	$2 billion	Large donor
George Soros	Hedge Fund Manager	$6.7 billion	Huge donor
Bill Gates	Investor	$130 billion	Donates to Democrats far more than to Republicans
Warren Buffett	Investor	$135 billion	He is a "Democrat." Endorsed Hillary Clinton in 2016

Oprah Winfrey	Producer	$3 billion	Large donor
Steve Ballmer	Investor	$123 billion	Large donor
Taylor	Singer	$1 billion	Endorses Democrats
Steven Spielberg	Director/Prod.	$4.8 billion	Large donor

Sources for Table No. 2. Forbes, MarketRealist.com, Wikipedia, Investipedia (net worth); E. Goldberg, "These Are the U. S. Billionaires Who Back Gun Control," *Forbes* June 15, 2016 (Bloomberg, Gates, Buffet, Oprah, Allen, Ballmer, Soros); M. Bernstein, Which Billionaire's Family is Helping Fund Oregon's Gun Control Ballot Measure?," OregonLive.com (Feb. 22, 2023) (Ballmer); "Anti-Gun Billionaire George Soros Pumps $18 Billion into His Political Apparatus," *Buckeye Firearms Association* (Nov. 1, 2017) (Soros); M. Muller, "Taylor Swift Supports Gun Control Without Making Any Political Statements," magazine.com (Mar. 23, 2018) (Swift); Steve Ballmer gives some donations to the Republicans. OpenSecrets.org, Reuters.com (Buffett); *Id.* (Gates, Conway and Spielberg), Wash. Post (Bloomberg donations), Giffords.org (Conway), https://www.reuters.com/article/idUSKCN1G42HX/ (Spielberg and Winfrey); OpenSecrets.org (Winfrey).

THE ONE BIG LIE

It is critical to understand the fundamental premise of the gun control movement. That premise is this: *because of the Second Amendment and the widespread legal availability of guns, the United States is a uniquely violent country.*

I will prove conclusively in this book that this is false, and I will do so by introducing two separate comprehensive statistics that are independent of each other and the accuracy of which cannot reasonably be disputed because each of the component parts of the two statistics is drawn from widely published sources that cannot reasonably be questioned.

What is the ultimate goal of the gun control movement? They will not tell you but I will. **They want all of your guns.** They want to ban all privately-owned guns, creating a government gun monopoly that will leave citizens completely at the mercy of the government. How do we know this? The gun control movement is philosophically and ideologically committed to creating a society where all civilian gun ownership has been banned and only the government can possess and use firearms. The only reason they don't admit this is that it would hurt them politically and engender tremendous resistance. Rather than be honest, they have adopted a strategy of Fabian incrementalism where a complete gun ban will be installed, piece by piece while we sleep, and when we finally realize what they are up to, it will be too late as we will no longer have the means to resist. To quote Richard II, "I wasted time and now doth time waste me." Since they will not admit their true intent, that intent must be inferred from a number of different facts.

Gun control is a *progressive* idea. The government can solve a social problem, violent crime, by using aggressive government force, that is, gun laws, law enforcement, arrests, prosecutions and ultimately incarceration for the recalcitrant. As I pointed out in *Progressivism: A Primer,* progressivism has no limiting principle; government will continually grow until it mollifies all the fear and anxiety that fuel the political psychotherapy of progressivism. Since human fear and anxiety know no limits and there are always additional anxieties to be calmed, *the idea of gun control itself has no limits* and gun control proposals will continue until, in utopian fashion, all gun crimes cease.

The gun control movement argues that more guns produce more crime.[21] That core belief implies the need to *ban all guns.* Gun controllers believe that "gun laws work," and that "weak gun safety laws are killing nearly 40,000 Americans every year."[22] The Giffords Law Center all but concedes my point: *"we won't stop* until we've put an end to this epidemic once and for all." (Emphasis added).[23] Though they won't openly admit that they oppose the Second Amendment, there is tremendous momentum to repeal it. A recent Google search for the exact phrase "repeal the Second Amendment" returned 430,000 hits. Six progressive judges—Stevens, Souter, Ginsburg, Breyer, Sotomayor and Kagan—sharply dissented in *Heller, McDonald* and *Bruen* and would *never* have endorsed the view that the Second Amendment protects an individual right to bear arms unconnected to the defunct militia.[24] Thus, their legal brain trust is already on record implicitly authorizing *a complete gun ban.*

---

[21] For the contrary view, see John Lott, *More Guns, Less Crime: Understanding Crime and Gun Control Laws,* (3rd ed. 2010).

[22] https://giffords.org/lawcenter/gun-laws/

[23] *Id.*

[24] Militias have been replaced by the National Guard, which the Founders would have considered a "select militia," a pejorative term to them.

The gun control movement universally argues that guns are not useful for self-defense and that a gun in the home is more likely to be used against you than for you.[25] That logic argues for a complete gun ban. Gun control advocates have repeatedly stated that widespread civilian gun ownership is a threat to democracy, a belief that in recent years has risen to the status of a sacred value to be protected at all costs including nullifying one of the Bill of Rights. See Chapter 2. Gun control advocates frequently praise countries with so few privately-owned guns that they might as well have none for any difference it makes.

Finally, "watch the hands, not the mouth." There are thousands of gun laws on the books. Each year, more laws are added. 103 new laws were added in 2023.[26] There are hundreds of proposals for new gun control laws. What is not said is more important than what is said. No gun control advocate has ever said, "this is the last law we will ever need; pass this and we are good forever." This Freudian slip shows their true agenda is to *ban all guns as soon as it is politically possible.*

Because like its parent progressivism, the idea of gun control has no limiting principle, the promise of the gun control movement to use government gun violence to achieve its goals, is essentially a blank check promising an ever-increasing amount of government gun violence *directly*, and by consolidating power in the central government and

---

[25] https://vpc.org/revealing-the-impacts-of-gun-violence/self-defense-gun-use/; David Studdert, "Owning Guns Puts People in Your Home at Greater Risk of Being Killed, New Study Shows," time.com (June 3, 2022).
[26] Giffords.org.

weakening the power of the people to resist, will also tend to increase government gun violence *indirectly* by encouraging massive and continual government growth. Thus, any notion of compromising with the gun control movement is doomed to fail as *they will never stop* until they have seized every single privately-owned gun in America. Indeed, that being the case, those who favor the human right of self-defense must stop playing defense and go on the offensive by rolling back existing gun control laws until the promise of the Second Amendment is achieved: constitutional carry in every state and nationally.

The security gate a half mile from one of Michael Bloomberg's many mansions

1.   The Two Big Lies

Americans are subjected to an endless stream of gun control propaganda funded by billionaires protected by armed guards and sophisticated security systems. That propaganda is designed to make us believe two separate but interrelated lies. The first lie is that gun violence in America is almost exclusively perpetrated by criminals, albeit with a small number of officer-involved shootings. The second lie is that America is, in comparison to the largest 165 countries on the planet, an unusually violent country. The alleged cause of both facts is the Second Amendment's right to bear arms and the solution is to repeal or nullify that right through legislation, court decision or administrative regulation.

Gun control propaganda is so effective that it has managed to convince groups that have been some of history's biggest victims of violence after being disarmed or while being unarmed to support stricter gun laws. A casual familiarity with the sad history of the human race should be sufficient to conclude that some of the biggest victims of the deprivation of the right to bear arms have been women, blacks and Jews (and racial, ethnic and religious minorities in general); however, polls and voting patterns show these groups tend to support gun control by large margins.[27] Particularly stunning is majority support among women to further disarm themselves in a dangerous world.

---

[27] A. Whitehead & S. Perry, "Gun Control in the Crosshairs: Christian Nationalism and Opposition to Stricter Gun Laws," *Sage Journals* (July 23, 2018).

Throughout human history; throughout *recent* human history and *currently,* women have been and are the victims of one of the most vile crimes human imagination can conjure: mass rape as a weapon of war, genocide and democide.[28] *No one needs guns more than women need guns!* See Table No. 3.

Table No. 3

The Greatest Story Rarely Told
Mass Rape as a Political Weapon

REGIME	YEARS	VICTIMS
Nazi Germany	1939-1945	No reliable estimate but a very large number
Imperial Japan	1937-1945	200,000
Soviet Union	1939-1945	2,000,000
Bangladesh	1971	200,000-400,000
Yugoslavia	1992-1995	60,000
Liberia	1989-2003	40,000

---

[28] A. Reid-Cunningham, (2008) "Rape as a Weapon of Genocide," *Genocide Studies and Prevention: An International Journal:* Vol. 3: Iss. 3: Article 4; L. Peltola, "Rape and Sexual Violence Used as a Weapon of War and Genocide" (2018). CMC Senior Theses.

Rwanda	**1994**	**100,000-250,000**
Sierra Leone	**1991-2002**	**60,000**
Sudan (Darfur)	**2003-2024**	**15,000**
DRCongo	**1998-2008**	**200,000**

Sources: A. Reid-Cunningham, Note 28, *supra;* L. Peltola, *supra;* Wikipedia

Every single complaint by gun control advocates about violence in the United States pertains to criminals (except for officer-involved shootings[29]). There is no pro-gun control analysis that includes all or most *government gun violence* or, ironically, fails to advocate *more* government gun violence as a "solution" to the gun violence problem. (In fact, a Google and social media search shows that the term "government gun violence" is barely in currency.) This is so obvious it does not require any proof; however, some examples will be helpful to illustrate the point.

CNN states: "Ubiquitous gun violence in the United States has left few places unscathed over the decades."[30] The

---

[29] Fatal officer involved shootings average about 1000 per year. *Source:*
https://www.statista.com/statistics/585152/people-shot-to-death-by-us-police-by-race/

[30]   https://www.cnn.com/2021/11/26/world/us-gun-culture-world-comparison-intl-cmd/index.html

article is based on research that excludes "state-sponsored violence."

The Chinese government, which, ironically is guilty of shooting unarmed protesters in Tiananmen Square, stated in a lengthy report: "Gun violence is a chronic disease in the United States. . . . Gun violence is one of the acutest social problems in the United States, with ramifications not only for the victims and their families, but also for the entire society and country. In addition to the casualties caused and the threat to public security, it has also resulted in enormous economic losses and social trauma for the nation."[31] Of course, China is talking about crime, not government. Its regime wants to denigrate the right to bear arms lest their own citizens get any dangerous ideas.

Senator Charles Schumer issued a press release on December 6, 2023, stating:

> "Here are the facts: the scourge of gun violence in America is a national crisis. The American people are sick and tired of enduring one mass shooting after another. They're sick and tired of vigils and moments of silence for family, friends, classmates, coworkers. Today, Democrats have moved to pass the Assault Weapons Ban, to help rid our streets of these deadly weapons. . . . We already have a decade's worth of proof that a ban on military-style

---

[31] Gun Violence in the United States: Truth and Facts 2023-02-16 (Ministry of Foreign Affairs).

assault weapons works and saves lives, plain and simple."[32]

The Senator is obviously not talking about government gun violence as the reference to banning "military-style assault weapons" shows. He is surely not for banning the government from having such weapons.

Another example illustrates the point. Daniel Semenza, Ph.D., published an article for the Rockefeller Institute.[33] He argues that "where there are more guns, there are more gun deaths." All references to gun violence in his article indicate he is talking about crime, not government action. Nowhere in his article does he allude to or recognize the massive number of acts of government gun violence that occur every year. He also states that America is a world leader in gun violence, however, he restricts his analysis to "high-income countries." Contradicting himself, however, he admits that gun violence in America is highest in low-income areas. He says nothing about the level of gun violence in higher-income, urban, suburban and rural areas where gun ownership is high. He also includes suicides that juice the number of "homicides," since the popular mind

---

[32] https://www.democrats.senate.gov/news/press-releases/majority-leader-schumer-floor-remarks-on-senate-republicans-blocking-passage-of-the-assault-weapons-ban-and-continuing-to-work-to-fight-the-national-crisis-of-gun-violence-in-america#

[33] "More Guns, More Death: The Fundamental Fact that Supports a Comprehensive Approach to Reducing Gun Violence in America," rockist.org (June 21, 2022).

conjures up only murder when that term is used.[34] And, of course, his analysis excludes non-gun violence which tends to further skew the numbers in favor of his argument.[35] However, most crimes of violence in the United States *do not* involve a gun.[36]

He saw fit to compare the United States with such alleged "peer countries" as Australia, Austria, Belgium, Czech Republic, Denmark, Finland, Greece, Hungary, Ireland, Korea, Netherlands, New Zealand, Norway, Portugal, Slovak Republic, Sweden, and Switzerland. Again, just as his analysis of the domestic front excludes government gun violence, so too his comparisons of the United States with other countries utilize only private gun violence statistics. He refers only once and briefly to one of the major causes of violence (excluding war) in the country and elsewhere: "The US . . . rate of firearm murders ranks roughly 30th in the world, exceeded almost exclusively by countries in South America ravaged by relentless drug wars." So anxious is he to use this fact to show the high level of gun violence in the United States that he seems oblivious to the fact that violence is related to the drug trade in countries that *consume* drugs as well as those that *produce* them. While gun control advocates gleefully include drug-related violence in their archives, statistics and arguments, they neglect to point out the obvious solution to drug-related

---

[34] See, R. McMaken, "Five Tricks Gun-Control Advocates Play," *Mises.org* (Nov. 1, 2016).

[35] *Id.*

[36] https://www.statista.com/statistics/251919/number-of-assaults-in-the-us-by-weapon/.

violence: ending the progressive Democratic drug war.[37] As a wealthy country that leads the world in illegal drug consumption,[38] the United States has a massive amount of drug-related violence.

The ideology of progressivism is deeply embedded in his article. Progressive policy failures need scapegoats. Guns are proffered as a scapegoat for problems actually caused in large part by failed government policies such as the drug war. The solution is always more government gun violence, illustrating that gun control advocates *exclude* government gun violence from their description of the problem to be solved.

My thesis is also confirmed by examining the solutions proffered by the major gun control groups. Everytown has a list of 47 alleged solutions including extreme risk laws, waiting periods, prohibiting open carry, and mandating permits for concealed carry.[39] Each of them addresses and seeks to reduce or restrict *private* gun ownership. None of them seeks to reduce *government gun violence*, indeed, most of their proposals will vastly increase such violence by creating ever more laws and regulations that must be enforced at government gunpoint. Obviously, the gun control movement is unconcerned about the massive number of powerful firearms that American governments possess and use on a daily basis.

---

[37] Ostrowski, James (1990) "The Moral and Practical Case for Drug Legalization," *Hofstra Law Review*: Vol. 18: Iss. 3, Article 5.

[38] https://www.cbsnews.com/news/us-leads-the-world-in-illegal-drug-use/

[39] https://www.everytown.org/solutions/

The Gun Violence Archive is a major website that tracks "gun violence." It claims to have adopted a broad, objective definition of gun violence:

> "Gun Violence describes the results of all incidents of death or injury or threat with firearms without pejorative judgment within the definition. Violence is defined without intent or consequence as a consideration. To that end a shooting of a victim by a subject/suspect is considered gun violence as is a defensive use or an officer involved shooting. The act itself, no matter the reason is violent in nature."[40]

However, it is clear from their charts, graphs and reports that the only type of government gun violence it tracks is officer involved shootings. It therefore fails to track or count any other form of government gun violence, including arrests and incarceration or any other form of threatened gun violence such as traffic stops. Thus, the gun control movement does believe and does state endlessly that the violence problem in America is almost exclusively a matter of crime. This is demonstrably false. See Chapter 2.

The second big lie of the gun control movement is often not stated directly but is inculcated indirectly by an endless series of half-truths and misleading statements and by leaving out large portions of the truth. It has often been stated that the best propaganda must be based on a kernel

---

[40] https://www.gunviolencearchive.org/methodology

of truth to convince the audience that it is credible. Propaganda has been defined as:

> "the systematic propagation of information or ideas by an interested party, specifically, in a tendentious (expressing or intending to promote a particular cause or point of view, especially a controversial one) way, in order to encourage or instill a certain attitude or response."[41]

I contend that the gun control movement, whether they explicitly say it or not, wants people to believe that *America is a uniquely or unusually violent country.* They accomplish this deft piece of propaganda by a variety of means that will be explored here. As I will prove in Chapter 3, this is false.

This startling assertion appears on the website of Everytown for Gun Safety: "The U.S. gun homicide rate is 26x higher than that of other high-income countries."[42] It cites to a dead link as the organization that did the study is now defunct. This is a brilliant piece of propaganda because, while it may literally be true, it is highly misleading and appears to be calculated to "encourage or instill a certain attitude or response"—that the United States is an extremely violent country. What they don't tell you is that the statistics *include* suicides and *exclude* homicides by means other than guns. Nor do they tell you which countries they are comparing the United States to. Nor do they explain the

---

[41] guides.lib.wayne.edu/c.php?g=401320&p=2729574

[42] everytown.org/debunking-gun-myths-at-the-dinner-table/

relationship between development and crime or how the number of guns explains the homicide rate. However, the desired result is achieved. Low information voters are led to believe that guns per se are the problem and gun control will solve the problem. The popularity of gun control in polling and the election of pro-gun control politicians shows that this propaganda works.

Advocates of gun control cherry-pick their data and studiously ignore all data that contradicts their position. For example, they were utterly silent about the disastrous consequences of strict gun control in Israel that allowed terrorists to massacre Israelis on October 7, 2023. They were likewise silent about the mass shooting at a concert in strict gun control Russia on March 22, 2024. Nor did they have any comments about Ecuador abandoning its strict gun control policies in the face of violence from gangs,[43] and Ukraine offering to distribute rifles to citizens to combat the Russian invasion.[44]

Instead of comparing the United States to *all* countries, they almost always limit their comparisons to "developed countries" or "high-income countries." They rarely explain why they exclude the other countries and rarely define their terms. As economist Ryan McMaken of the Mises Institute explains, "the whole notion of the 'developed' world creates

---

[43]   https://www.reuters.com/world/americas/ecuadors-lasso-authorizes-civilian-use-guns-citing-insecurity-2023-04-02/

[44]   https://www.indiatoday.in/world/russia-ukraine-war/story/ukraine-russian-invasion-war-crisis-ukranian-army-assault-rifles-vladimir-putin-volodymyr-zelenskyy-1917607-2022-02-25

an arbitrary line between numerous high-middle income countries and a small number of the wealthiest countries."[45] This arbitrary classification, however, allows the gun control movement to cherry-pick its data by comparing the United States, a diverse country with the third largest population on Earth, with a long list of mostly small, monocultural European countries. This is absurd on its face. The division between developed and undeveloped countries has been the subject of criticism for years as being arbitrary and the World Bank discontinued using the term in 2016.[46] Being useful for propaganda, however, the gun control movement continues to use the term.

Worse yet, this endless and baseless comparison between the United States and a set of mostly contiguous, monocultural European countries is a mistake for another reason. The violent crime problem in the United States is clearly centered in the African-American community which has a unique history of gross mistreatment by British colonial and American governments for 405 years and *continuing*. African-Americans suffered first through slavery, then Jim Crow and Black Codes and then through a series of failed and discriminatory policies, sometimes well-intentioned but often not, from the whole period from the end of slavery (1865) through the present time and continuing. The author published a monograph on this subject entitled, *Progressive Big Government's War on Black People* (1865-2021).[47] The book explains that:

---

[45] "Five Tricks Gun-Control Advocates Play," *Mises.org* (Nov. 1, 2016).
[46] *Source*: Wikipedia.
[47] See also, Walter Williams, *The State Against Blacks* (1982).

"After slavery, the government never got off the backs of the freed slaves and their descendants. Indeed, with each passing generation, additional government policies kept putting more and more roadblocks in the path of black people—Jim Crow, black codes, the racist policies of the Progressive Era, the discriminatory policies and huge taxes of the New Deal, the union and wage policies explicitly designed to hurt blacks in the job market; the war on drugs, which disproportionately hurt blacks systematically shut out of the economy and often leaving the drug trade as their best option; the war on guns, explicitly designed to prevent blacks from protecting themselves from racist terrorist groups and from the government itself; the Great Society, which did what slavery failed to do, break up the black family—according to Jason Riley, 'Only 16 percent of black families are married couples with children'; LBJ's Vietnam War, which hit blacks hard as they could not finagle their way around the draft, killing thousands and leaving tens of thousands addicted to heroin and doomed to a hopeless life when they returned to America; government schools, often explicitly created or operated on racist grounds to disadvantage black kids but forcing black taxpayers to pay for them anyway."

Significantly, through their entire history and continuing, *African-Americans were systemically disarmed*, or harder hit by later gun control laws than other Americans with the result that, by all accounts, they have fewer guns than other Americans, not more. It is therefore difficult to argue that the greater degree of violence in this community is the result of the greater availability of guns when other communities have more guns and less crime.

Because of the unique and tragic history of African-Americans in the United States, with many continuing traumas that to this day tend to produce more crime, unqualified comparisons of the violent crime rate between the United States and European countries are extremely misleading. If underdeveloped countries tend to be more violent, as the gun controllers imply, they should be willing to acknowledge that *underdeveloped areas inside the United States* may also be violent and guns are simply a scapegoat to avoid addressing the real problems. None of the so-called developed or high-income countries has had the equivalent of a captive nation embedded within their borders for the last 405 years.

Ironically, as previously stated, the gun control movement is essentially identical to the Democratic Party, which claims to have the best interests of the black community at heart. At the same time, since gun control is a form of scapegoating that covers up the true nature of the problems underlying violence, blaming pieces of metal for the historical and structural problems in the black community, like all forms of scapegoating, merely serves to cover up and ignore the real, underlying problems, in my view, involving *405 years of being victimized by government gun violence,* a lack of local control,[48] a myriad of failed progressive policies and of course, being systematically disarmed of the means to defend themselves. *Amazingly, the whole gun control movement essentially rests on this grossly mistaken comparison to European countries!*

Here is a typical MSM media article about guns:

> "Ubiquitous gun violence in the United States has left few places unscathed over the decades. Still, many Americans hold their right to bear arms, enshrined in the US Constitution, as sacrosanct. But critics of the Second Amendment say that right threatens another: The right to life. America's relationship to gun ownership is unique, and *its gun culture is a global outlier.* As the tally of gun-related deaths continue to grow daily, here's a look at how gun culture in the US compares to the rest of the world. . . .The United States is the only nation in the world where civilian guns outnumber people."[49] (Emphasis added)

Again, without making too many obviously false statements, the *impression* this statement makes is that America is a uniquely violent country because of the Second

---

[48] Several large cities have black mayors, however, most of the policies that afflict the cities are decided on the federal and state level.

[49] "How US gun culture stacks up with the world," <u>CNN.com</u> (Feb. 15, 2024).

Amendment. The article repeats gun control propaganda virtually verbatim: "The US has the highest firearm homicide rate in the developed world." The article also compares so-called "mass shootings" and suicides in gross numbers and not per capita, ignoring the fact that the United States is the third largest country in the world.

Here is yet another classic instance of gun control propaganda from the Washington Post: "The United States is the only country in the world where mass shootings regularly occur."[50] Again, this statement contains a kernel of truth but serves to seriously mislead the reader. First, it ignores the sheer size of the United States and uses raw numbers as opposed to numbers adjusted for the size of countries. Second, it ignores mass killings by other means such as stabbings and arson which are common in the world. Third, the author of course ignores any type of violence other than crime, however, the world is replete with mass shootings on a daily basis in wars, civil wars, guerrilla wars and by means of democide and terrorism. All these factors are considered in this book.

Of all of the gun control groups, Brady: United Against Gun Violence, is the most forthright about defining their view of the gun problem in America, *and confirming the thesis of this chapter:* "Gun violence is a uniquely American crisis." Note that in this formulation, any qualifiers about comparing us only with "developed countries" or "peer countries" or "high-income countries" are absent. It is not common for a gun control group to so blatantly announce their propaganda.

---

[50] M. Flynn, "Virginia Democrats explain their positions on gun policies," *Washington Post* (June 17, 2022).

The phrase "the United States is the only country …" is extremely common in gun control propaganda, usually followed by a statement about how we have more guns than people or the most mass shootings. The endless use of that phrase serves to reinforce the false notion that the United States is a uniquely or unusually violent country. Endless repetition of falsehoods is a standard feature of successful political propaganda.

For decades now, the gun control movement, along with their allies in the media and in the schools and colleges, have bombarded the public with a steady stream of highly misleading propaganda all aiming at the inculcation of the belief that the United States is a uniquely or unusually violent country. The remainder of this book will disprove this propaganda once and for all.

2.   The Government is the Biggest Perpetrator of Gun Violence in the United States

MEASURING GOVERNMENT GUN VIOLENCE

The first statistic introduced in this book will prove conclusively that the number one cause and number one perpetrator of gun violence in the United States by far is the government itself. When I say, "by far", I mean *astronomically* by far. Since this is the case and since the gun control movement seeks to massively increase that amount of violence through each and every one of its proposals, the whole notion that the gun control movement could possibly reduce gun violence is absurd. *It will astronomically increase gun violence both directly and indirectly.*

How do we prove that the leading perpetrator of gun violence in the United States is the government itself? Let's compare private gun violence with government gun violence.

There are about 1.2 million violent crimes in the country each year.[51] Most of them *do not* involve the use of a firearm. Taking 2019 as a baseline, criminals commit about 285,000 gun crimes of violence each year in the United States.[52] Let's consider those 285,000 gun crimes. Each one by definition is an example of the failure of government to fulfill its

---

[51] Source: ucr.fbi.gov.

[52] Sources: FBI UCI; Bureau of Justice Statistics, National Crime Victimization Survey, 1993-2001.

promise to provide law and order, its only real valid purpose. (See below in this chapter.). The failure of the government to deter crime is not an argument for gun control but for the right to bear arms. Second, many of those crimes were the direct or indirect result of numerous failed government policies such as the war on drugs. Finally, many of the victims were unarmed and no doubt a large percentage were unarmed because they had been disarmed by the government!

The quantity of government violence is nearly impossible to measure. The sheer variety of such violence is daunting for any honest researcher. The government stalks and watches you everywhere you go on CCTV, hacks your computers and smart phones, tortures prisoners, executes innocent people, terrorizes people with thousands of laws they never heard of, forces vaccinations, kidnaps your kids (government schools), bombs civilians, engages in endless war with hundreds of military bases in dozens of foreign countries,[53] conducts illegal searches, seizures and break-ins at all hours, conscripts soldiers in times of war, verbally abuses citizens and makes violent threats, seizes private property (tax foreclosures, forfeiture and eminent domain), compels jury duty, engages in a war on drug users, manufacturers and sellers, engages in a war on gun owners, manufacturers and sellers, blocks roads, engages in police

---

[53]   https://www.cato.org/commentary/750-bases-80-countries-too-many-any-nation-time-us-bring-its-troops-home

brutality, has 1419 nuclear weapons on high alert,[54] has millions of weapons including machine guns and drones, billions of rounds of ammunition, has portable tax collectors patrolling the highways, the world's largest prison population, 100's of victimless crime laws, 100 different taxes and fees (theft), and 10,000 "regulations" (acts of violence against peaceful people). This clever abuser, through Stockholm Syndrome [55] and almost complete control over "education," has managed to convince most of its victims that there has been no abuse or that it's their own fault! When confronted, this perpetrator denies any violence or abuse and blames the victims! To overcome all this gaslighting we need only to open our eyes, take the blinders off and see what is in front of our faces.

We can divide government gun violence into actual and threatened, although the lines can get blurry. Also, many acts of government gun violence are *continuing* in nature, such as arrests and imprisonment, raising the essentially metaphysical question of whether these constitute a single act of violence or whether each day, hour or even moment constitutes a separate and distinct act of violence. Surely, being falsely imprisoned for twenty years is worse than being wrongly detained on the street for ten minutes, yet, I am aware of no means of calculating such acts of violence. I propose that since being detained is a massive violation of

----

[54]

https://www.armscontrol.org/factsheets/Nuclearweapons whohaswhat

[55]   https://www.webmd.com/mental-health/what-is-stockholm-syndrome

liberty in and of itself and also involves an implied threat of *deadly physical force* if the prisoner were to resist, that, at a minimum, for statistical purposes, *each additional hour* of such detention must be counted as a separate and distinct act of violence. Thus, a single person imprisoned for five years for an imaginary crime such as possessing private property[56] (drugs) or exercising his right to bear arms (gun possession) or for money possession (tax evasion, money laundering) can be justly said to have been victimized 43,800 times! Since the Progressive State of America leads the world in incarceration,[57] it therefore engages in so many acts of violence that calculating the precise number seems unnecessary if the point of the exercise is to compare the number of acts of government gun violence to the number of acts of private gun violence (a mere 285,000 annually).[58] Let's just say it is astronomical squared. Nevertheless, let us catalog as best we can the amazing number of acts of government gun violence each year in the United States.

Arrests—7 million x each hour of detention[59]

Prison incarceration—1.8 million x each hour of the day[60]

Jury summonses—32 million a year[61]

---

[56] Thomas Szasz, *Our Right to Drugs: The Case for a Free Market* (1996).

[57] WorldPopulationReview.com.

[58] *Source:* ucr.fbi.gov.

[59] *Source:* statista.com.

[60] *Source:* prisonstudies.org.

[61] *Source:* National Center for State Courts.

Traffic stops (portable tax collection)—20 million a year, mostly to raise revenue[62]

Threats of traffic stops—astronomical

Tax deadlines and tax bills and notices—local, state and federal—astronomical

Tax foreclosures—tens of thousands (no hard data is available)

Selective Service Registration—millions each year

The Lockdown—two years of barring travel and public assembly, forcing businesses to close, forcing people to wear masks, and stealing trillions to subsidize the closing of the economy—literally **billions** of individual acts of aggression all backed up with government guns.

Compulsory schooling—80 million parents are forced to send their 40 million children to government school 180 days a year. Do the math. That's 21.6 **trillion** threats of government gun violence each year (counting days only, not hours).

Forfeiture of private property—thousands each year[63]

Courthouse searches—millions each year

Border searches—millions each year

---

[62] *Source:* https://openpolicing.stanford.edu/findings/. Note how little traffic enforcement there is during rush hour and how many speed traps there are on weekend mornings and in the middle of nowhere during the day in perfect weather. Why? It's easier get a good radar hit at those times!

[63] James Bovard, "Highway Robbery Continues to be the Law of the Land," <u>LewRockwell.com</u> (Feb. 28, 2024).

Road blocks—thousands each year affecting hundreds of people each[64]
Eminent Domain seizures—thousands each year

These are just some of the many sources of actual or threatened government gun violence or at least the palpable threat of such violence. The point I hope has been made.

Most government gun violence involves *threats* so let's consider threatened violence. You can't compare *private* threats of gun violence with *governmental* threats of gun violence as one is instantaneous and the other is continuous and essentially permanent. If you are a bank teller and a robber comes in demanding money and starts reaching for what appears to be a gun, you may be under threat of being shot for a minute or so. If you are being incarcerated for an imaginary crime,[65] you are under threat of being shot for escaping 24/7/365. There is no comparison between the two. Implicit threatened government violence is astronomically more damaging than momentary private threats of gun violence.

Support for my view that threats of gun violence must be part of any social calculus of violence appears to come from an unlikely source. Professor Michael Ulrich, a supporter of gun control, in a recent article, makes a number

---

[64] In my view, roadblocks are illegal general searches under the Fourth Amendment. These are precisely the kind of obnoxious search common during the Colonial period that led to the drafting of the Fourth Amendment in the first place.

[65] A crime with no victim as no force or fraud was involved.

of interesting observations. He states that "police shootings are gun violence." Elsewhere, he writes:

> "Guns can also generate harm without a trigger ever being pulled. Firearms can be used for threats and intimidation, for example, to perpetuate sexual violence and psychological torment. Police shootings can generate anxiety, post-traumatic stress disorder, feelings of helplessness and fear. Gun violence from law enforcement may even be a contributor to elevated rates of preterm delivery and cardiovascular disease in Black women. Long-term effects on youth may not be fully understood for years, but it should be unacceptable that a majority of high school students report concerns that a shooting will take place in their school or community."[66]

Though Professor Ulrich would likely disagree with the thrust of this book, if he agrees that police *shootings* are gun violence and agrees that *threats* of gun violence are also gun violence, he would presumably agree with me that threats of government violence must be accounted for in any calculus of overall violence in society.

Every day, each citizen is subject to an implied threat to enforce hundreds of different laws, the violation of which involves intrinsically peaceful behavior. These include at least fifty different taxes, thousands of regulations and

---

[66] M. Ulrich, "Finding Balance in the Fight Against Gun Violence," *J Law Med Ethics.* 2023 Spring; 51(1): 7–13.

hundreds of crimes, defined in local, county, state and federal statutes, codes and ordinances, the entirety of which no human has ever read.[67] In *Progressivism: A Primer,* I explored the far-reaching and long-term consequences of living under the constant strain of state coercion:

> "Since the very function of aggressive force in human affairs is to negate the use of the victim's rational mind in determining how his life, liberty and property are to be utilized, progressivism also moves away from the use of reason in human life. This harsh truth can be seen from the perspectives of the progressive and the progressive's victims. Progressives, having government guns at their disposal, need not spend time or energy developing rational arguments that would appeal to the minds of their victims as to the value of the various goals they wish to achieve. Government guns make that unnecessary and even silly. When is the last time you had a philosophical debate with a cop or an IRS agent?

> "The victim of progressive barbarism also is hindered in the full use of his rational mind. Instead of using his rational mind to determine how his life, liberty and property are to be utilized, he must instead be concerned with how to comply with the virtually limitless

---

[67] Harvey A. Silverglate, *Three Felonies a Day: How the Feds Target the Innocent* (2009).

number of threats of violence progressive government aims at him. Thus, citizens of the Progressive State of America live in a perpetual state of fear of being punished for violating edicts whose purpose either has never been explained to them or whose rationale they have

This photo of a small portion of a law library depicts more law books than most people could read in a lifetime. *Credit:* photograph in the Carol M. Highsmith Archive, Library of Congress, Prints and Photographs Division.

never accepted or even have concluded is complete nonsense."[68]

If you multiply the number of citizens by the number of implied threats and by the number of days in the year, you end up with the kind of numbers only a math PhD could grasp. More than the grains of sand on the beach? More than the stars in the sky? Who knows?

I have thrown a lot of numbers around. Does the government commit tens of millions of acts of violence each year or is it billions, trillions or even *quadrillions*? What difference does it make? I have proven my point that *the government itself is the leading cause of gun violence in America*. The number of discrete acts of gun violence government actors commit against peaceful victims is astronomically higher than the piddling number of private sector crimes the government fails to stop each year, most of which are causally related to failed progressive big government programs anyway. I have expatiated on such criminogenic policies in my books including *Political Class Dismissed* ("Our Urban Policies are a Real Riot"). They include failed welfare programs, the failed drug war and failed economic policies that keep the poor, poor, generation after generation.

Private sector violence (crime) is far less frequent than public sector violence and usually lasts a brief period while government violence in the form of threats is much longer lasting in duration. People can take precautions against *private* violence, however, *government* gun violence is *inescapable* and continuous, like a life sentence in an open-air prison. To combat this massive edifice of *continual violence from*

---

[68] Pp. 63-64.

birth to death, you are given exactly one vote for either of two parties *both of which support the present regime.* In 2020, 158,074,641 Americans voted for President. Thus, if you voted that year, you got a 1/158,074,641 share of the say over a government that has 100 percent control over you.

The alleged opposition party, the Republicans, have not repealed a single major progressive program since the beginning of the Progressive Era in 1913. Thus, since 1913 and currently, your one vote is almost certainly *never going to make even a slight difference in the level of government violence you suffer under in your lifetime.* Voting is like trying to stop a hurricane with your breath. As I explained in *Progressivism A Primer,*[69] its main practical purpose is to rationalize the government's use of violence against you. That is what democracy looks like.

REFUTING THE CONSENT ARGUMENT

The first line of defense against the very notion of government violence is based on consent. It's not violence at all because in America, government is based on the consent of the governed. Libertarians[70] both historical and contemporary have spent a considerable amount of time showing this argument is utter nonsense. They include Lysander Spooner (1808-1887), whose work is being revived by an attorney/podcaster known as "Legalman" on

---

[69] *Progressivism: A Primer on the Idea Destroying America* (2014).

[70] The term "libertarian" used in this book means a person who believes that individual liberty is the highest political value. See, Lew Rockwell, "What Libertarianism Is, and Isn't," <u>LewRockwell.com</u> (March 31, 2014)

Twitter/X, law professor Randy Barnett and this author as well in *Progressivism: A Primer* which summarizes Barnett's work. [71] The libertarians instead assert that American government is based on coercion (violence), not consent.

Suffice it to say here there is zero evidence that any American explicitly consented to being ruled by the government from birth to death in every aspect of their lives on pain of being killed or imprisoned for decades if not life if they resist. There is simply no evidence for this silly proposition. Rather, the notion that American government is based on the consent of the governed relies on the notion of *implied consent.* However, that argument fares no better. The fatal flaw in all implied consent theories is this: for a valid implied consent to be found, there must be a way *not to consent* and there never is.[72] For example, if you vote, you consent; if you don't vote, you consent since you could have voted. All arguments for implied consent are not arguments at all but attempts to rationalize a conclusion already reached for ideological reasons. Many intellectuals in America love powerful, centralized progressive big government and use illusory consent as a lazy way of justifying their preexisting ideological predilections. They will have to do better.

AMERICAN DEMOCRACY IS A SHAM

In the absence of any actual argument for democracy and in the absence of any evidence that Americans consented to the regime, I suppose the regime's court

---

[71] See, *Progressivism: A Primer*, pp. 32-33; Randy Barnett, *Restoring the Constitution* (2004).
[72] *Id.*

intellectuals will fall back on some notion that government violence is legitimate because the people are allowed to vote in elections and thus they participate *to some extent* in enacting the policies that government violence enforces. This is basically smuggling back into the argument a kind of a fuzzy, backdoor collective notion of consent. Even if democracy *in theory* justifies government violence beyond the defense function, it must still be proven that *American* democracy as it currently functions provides Americans with whatever degree of choice of policies that justifies the massive violence they suffer under at all times. The fact remains, no valid argument for this position has been made. As I have explained elsewhere, there are numerous and insuperable structural flaws in electoral politics that render the average American voter essentially powerless to affect government policy.

If you look at how American electoral politics actually operates,[73] you see no evidence that American democracy

---

[73] The author has 54 years experience in electoral politics, including involvement in both major parties and several minor parties. He has been a candidate, campaign manager, paid consultant, election lawyer and volunteer for dozens of campaigns. He has done election law litigation for decades and has represented Dr. Ron Paul when he ran for President, the Libertarian Party, the Conservative Party and the Green Party. See *Libertarian Party of N.Y. v. N.Y. State Bd. of Elections,* 22-44-cv (2nd Cir. 2022). In that case, the Green Party and Libertarian Party had earned ballot access by meeting the legal standard, but had their status removed after the fact by legislation. We lost the appeal and they were kept off the

allows average citizens sufficient control over the government to justify the massive amount of government violence they must endure every day of their lives. It would take a book-length treatment to do the subject justice, so the case can only be summarized here. My books *Political Class Dismissed* and *Progressivism: A Primer* discuss these issues in detail.

American politics is dominated almost completely by special interest groups that are the source of the lion's share of donations. I once did a study of who made large donations to politicians in Erie County, New York (Buffalo).[74] Unsurprisingly, almost every single large donor had a major personal stake in the outcome of the election. Over time, these donors were then richly rewarded by the politicians they installed with various forms of legalized graft such as loans, special tax breaks and government grants. The report is worth quoting at length:

> "What we found was that a small number of persons contribute gargantuan sums of money to candidates, parties and committees. The largest contributors in our preliminary analysis were owners and executives of large corporations. . . . There is a clear pattern to

ballot. So much for democracy. If you are not part of the two-party duopoly, you get crushed!

[74] https://web.archive.org/web/20110719033621/http://freenewyork.org/articles/newsalerts/Free New York News Alert No. 11--Who Runs Buffalo.pdf.

their contributions. While there are exceptions to the rule, a large portion of the contributions is given to party committees or to incumbents running for re-election. Party affiliation matters less than incumbency. Thus, these large contributions help to maintain the status quo in Buffalo area politics. On the rare occasions when incumbents are seriously challenged, the critical difference has often been these large contributions. More importantly, the large campaign war chests the incumbents build up discourage serious challengers in the first place. That is why many incumbents run unopposed or with only token opposition from 'sacrificial lambs.' Thus, in seeking a true answer to the question: 'Who runs Buffalo?'--we are led, not to the Democratic Party or the Republican Party, but to the Big Business Party and its platform: the maintenance of the status quo."

The report further noted who did and who did not donate to campaigns:

"Political donors tend to be drawn from the following groups: wealthy businessmen; firms that do large amounts of work with governments or are heavily regulated: banking, insurance, real estate, engineering, architecture, construction, health care, law (large corporate firms and personal injury firms), unions, politicians themselves, government employees.

In short, there is one term that encompasses them all: *special interest group.* Each of these groups has interests special to themselves and adverse to the general interests of average citizens. Average citizens of modest means who do not fall within one of these categories rarely contribute and when they do, it is often based on a personal friendship or family relation and the sums they contribute are small. They are not a major factor in politics."

Thus, the average anonymous citizen with an anonymous single vote is no match for publicly identified large donors in influencing politicians and policy.

My own research is strongly corroborated by a major study that concluded that American government is not a democracy at all but essentially an oligarchy. The study concluded:

"Despite the seemingly strong empirical support in previous studies for theories of majoritarian democracy, our analyses suggest that *majorities of the American public actually have little influence over the policies our government adopts.* Americans do enjoy many features central to democratic governance, such as regular elections, freedom of speech and association, and a widespread (if still contested) franchise. But we believe that if policymaking is dominated by powerful business organizations and a small number of affluent Americans, then America's claims to being a democratic society are seriously threatened."[75]

It is important to point out that this study concluded that voters *in the majority* have little actual say in policy. *A fortiori,* voters not in the majority or voters in the extreme minority have even less influence on policy and thus the coercion they are subject to is *not* morally justified by the provision to them of illusory choices.

The domination of politics by political machines and special interest groups is another nail in the coffin of democracy. Here, the concept of rational apathy comes into play.[76] In short, the incentive some people have to grow the government is stronger than the incentive most people have to stop them because the benefits to members of a special interest group, which could be millions or billions of dollars, are greater than the incentive the general public has to stop them. Fighting the sugar quota, for example, might cost a citizen $1000 at least with no guarantee of success, but the net benefit to that person if successful might be $25, meaning a net loss of $975. So, sugar subsidies worth billions continue.

Political machines are a type of special interest group. A machine is a cohesive group of people working toward the goal of increasing their own power and wealth at the expense

---

[75] M. Giles & B. Page, "Testing Theories of American Politics: Elites, Interest Groups, and Average Citizens," Cambridge University Press: 18 September 2014.
[76] A concept associated with the Public Choice School of economics.

of *everyone* else in the community. Machines, being small numbers of highly-disciplined and highly motivated people, almost always are able to defeat the disorganized, leaderless and poorly motivated masses. Generations of reformers, including the author, have tried for many decades to defeat machines and drive policy by some concept of the public or general interest and we have failed because the defects in the system that allow machines to operate are structural and almost impossible to eradicate. Reformers often score a few small victories in the short-term, but facing their inevitable defeat by the machine, almost always give up and join the machine themselves. Hence, my aphorism of politics: *all reformers become hacks.* The unifying theme here is this: those who control the government *now*—machines and special interests and the current bureaucracy—monetize their control of the government to politically defeat newcomers and challengers. This explains the legendary rate of incumbents being re-elected. Congressmen and state legislators are re-elected about 90 percent of the time.[77]

It should be noted that the notion that voting has value in the sense that voters can get together as a group and affect policy is negated by the domination of politics by machines and special interests. As previously argued, these relatively small but cohesive groups are generally able to outmaneuver the disorganized, demoralized, burned-out and leaderless masses. Thus, the notion is that government violence is justified because, in theory, the individual can go out and somehow figure out how to get millions of other people

---

[77]   opensecrets.org/elections-overview/reelection-rates; https://ballotpedia.org/Election results, 2022: Incumbent win rates by state

motivated and organized and coordinated to somehow defeat the professional political operatives in electoral battle. This is a pure drug-induced hallucination, not an argument. Of course, it is worth noting that once we leave the realm of *individual consent* and force people to recruit others to get their own way, the original, valid notion of consent consistent with *individual* natural rights has already been destroyed. Consent is only meaningful at the individual level because only individuals have rights.

There are many other flaws in democracy that serve to deprive voters of a meaningful choice over the policies that are forced upon them. Government controls most of the schools where future voters form their views of government. Those not controlled *directly*, K-12 government schools and state colleges and universities, are controlled *indirectly* by government subsidies, grants and loans. This obvious question is rarely asked: *how can you have fair elections when the government itself controls the inculcation of political ideas?* It is no accident that young people tend to vote for the party that is perceived to favor more government, the Democrats, while older voters, whose life experience may override the propaganda of their youth, are more likely to favor the party perceived to be for smaller government, the Republicans. (The fact that the GOP is itself a big government party is beside the point here.)

As if these major flaws in the system weren't enough, there are several more flaws in the political process that vitiate choice. In America for well over 100 years, politics has been dominated by two major parties that agree on most major issues. Your choice is limited to these two parties whose main policies are similar. Thus, democracy gives you an illusory choice of what's on its limited menu. If what you want is not on the menu, it's your tough luck.

Yet another flaw in democracy is the complete absence of any consideration of *cost* in the voting process. Voters are free to vote for any candidate they believe will advance any program regardless of the cost of that program. Since costs are real and must be taken account of in any rational choice outside the voting booth, it is difficult to see how voting expresses the actual realistic preferences of the voter. Voting does not really express your choices since it is cost-free and thus tends to produce bizarre results such as enacting welfare programs with $73 trillion in unfunded liabilities. [78] A decision-making process which allows people to completely ignore costs is absurd.

Advocates of democracy rarely address yet another major flaw in the process: tribal voting. Voters tend to vote for their perceived ethnic, religious and tribal interests. This is obvious to anyone who has seriously studied election results in the United States and elsewhere. This creates numerous problems but let's focus on the ramifications of this dynamic on the argument that voting provides voters with meaningful choices. If you are in the group majority, yet choose to vote on policy or philosophy or any other non-tribal factor, your vote is negated by tribal voting. Worse yet, if you are in the minority group, once again your choice will be negated by forces completely out of your control.

Let's dispatch the silly "argument" that every once in a great while, always for a minor local office, some politician beats another politician by one vote. First, this happens so

---

[78] https://www.cato.org/blog/medicare-social-security-are-responsible-100-percent-us-unfunded-obligations

rarely that it does not refute the obvious fact that 99.99% of the time, your one vote is meaningless. But even in those rare instances, the real question is not whether your one vote changed the result of one election but rather, did your one vote change any policies that actually improved your life? Let's say the odds of that happening are astronomical.

Gerrymandering is yet another chronic problem in democracies as Murray Rothbard explains:

> "The party in power at the time of division, or redivision, will inevitably alter the districts to produce a systematic bias in its favor; but no other way is inherently more rational or more truly evocative of majority will. Moreover, the very division of the earth's surface into countries is itself arbitrary. If a government covers a certain geographical area, does "democracy" mean that a majority group in a certain district should be permitted to secede and form its own government, or to join another country? Does democracy mean majority rule over a larger, or over a smaller, area? In short, which majority should prevail? The very concept of a national democracy is, in fact, self-contradictory. For if someone contends that the majority in Country X should govern that country, then it could be argued with equal validity that the majority of a certain district within Country X should be allowed to govern itself and secede from the larger country, and this subdividing process can

logically proceed down to the village block, the apartment house, and, finally, each individual, thus marking the end of all democratic government through reduction to individual self-government. But if such a right of secession is denied, then the national democrat must concede that the more numerous population of other countries should have a right to outvote his country; and so he must proceed upwards to a world government run by a world majority rule. In short, the democrat who favors national government is self-contradictory; he must favor a world government or none at all."[79]

Who gets to vote (age, citizenship status, felons), in what districts, who counts the votes and how can we be assured of an accurate vote count are all structural problems inherent in democracy to which no easy solution exists. Can the government "elect a new electorate" through mass immigration? Apparently so. The United States went from a center-right country in 1984 where Ronald Reagan won 49 states to the last four elections in a row where Republicans lost the so-called popular vote, not because progressive ideas got any better but largely because of immigration.

For years, Democrats complained about the unfairness of elections in spite of many prior episodes of alleged vote-rigging by the Democrats themselves. Then, all of a sudden, a miracle occurred. An election was held in 2020 in the midst of political violence, a sharply divided country, a Lockdown

---

[79] Murray Rothbard, *Power and Market* (2nd Ed, 1977), p. 192.

and massive and sudden changes in voting procedures, and yet, in spite of all that, it was such a perfect election with *zero* fraud that anyone who disagreed became a thought criminal banished from social media and even prosecuted! Yet, in a world where people will steal a bag of potato chips, why shouldn't we believe that people would also try to steal an election which determines the control of *trillions* of dollars and the fate of war and peace in the world? Fair elections require freedom of speech, yet it is clear that in 2020, *the government* conspired with social media to suppress supporters of one candidate so as to favor another.

Even if there was no voter fraud whatsoever and all votes were accurately counted, the 2020 election was nevertheless tainted. In his book, *Neither Fair Nor Free*, Joel Pollak writes:

> "The U. S. Presidential election in 2020 was distorted in ways that made it very difficult, if not impossible, for President Donald J. Trump to win re-election. Even without voter fraud— which, as of this writing, remains unproven— the conditions of the election violated the 'free and fair' standard."

He goes on to list a myriad of defects in the election, again, *leaving aside the issue of actual voter fraud.* These include, changing the system of voting in the midst of the election to favor one side, political violence, "censorship" of social media to favor one side, manipulation of search results, suppression of the Hunter Biden laptop story and false claims of "Russia collusion," rigged debates, obvious media bias and biased polling.

Let's close out this litany of irreparable and insuperable flaws in the argument that democracy provides people with real choice and control over their lives with this *coup de grace*: Let's say you overcome all the other obstacles in your path to control your life with your single vote for one of the limited choices on the menu over which you have zero control. You vote for the guy who promises X and he manages to win. What do you do if he changes his mind and fails to fulfill his campaign promise? I note this happens constantly in politics. In fact, there is *nothing* you can do. You have no recourse whatsoever, no legal or political remedy at all. The democrat[80] will say with a straight face, "You can vote against him the next time," oblivious to the fact that he just consigned you to an infinite regress of absurdity.

The final fatal flaw in *representative* democracy is this. Your "representative," who does not even know who you are or how you secretly voted and why, is *not* your representative, not your agent and not your fiduciary. He does not work for you and you cannot fire him. These are childish political myths and propaganda. He is a free agent who can do whatever he damn well pleases and is highly likely to win re-election anyway as generations of promise-breaking politicians have proven. The classic example is John McCain voting against repealing Obamacare after promising to repeal it when he ran for re-election.[81] Lysander Spooner put it this way:

---

[80] Person who favors majority rule.

[81] https://www.nbcnews.com/health/obamacare/mccain-hated-obamacare-he-also-saved-it-n904106#

"There are only certain men, who call themselves presidents, senators, and representatives, and claim to be the authorized agents, for the time being, or for certain short periods, of all 'the people of the United States;' but who can show no credentials, or powers of attorney, or any other open, authentic evidence that they are so; and who notoriously are not so; but are really only the agents of a secret band of robbers and murderers, whom they themselves do not know, and have no means of knowing, individually; but who, they trust, will openly or secretly, when the crisis comes, sustain them in all their usurpations and crimes."[82]

Yet another problem for democratic theory is how do democrats reconcile majority rule with the Bill of Rights? How do they reconcile majority rule with *any* constitution at all that restrains majority rule? If majority rule is the ultimate principle, how do democrats justify carving out certain rights that the majority cannot violate? Libertarians have no such conundrum because they propounded the doctrine of natural rights in the first place and helped craft the Bill of Rights largely based on natural rights philosophy which is, by its very nature, *undemocratic.*

Elections are a clumsy decision-making technology that replace a far more efficient technology of choice, the

---

[82] Lysander Spooner, *No Treason. No. VI. The Constitution of No Authority* (Boston: Published by the Author, 1870).

market.[83] Thus, every time the government takes over a previously free aspect of society, the average person's ability to make free choices is drastically reduced from near-total control to essentially zero control. That is what democracy looks like. Thus, libertarians do not complain about democracy because it gives people too much control over their lives and we would prefer an authoritarian regime that told them what to do and made them do it. On the contrary; we criticize democracy for not giving people enough control over their lives. Indeed, we contend that democracy gives them essentially *zero* control over their lives and thus, as Aldous Huxley predicted, democracy becomes an extremely insidious form of well-disguised *authoritarianism*:

> "By means of ever more effective methods of mind-manipulation, the democracies will change their nature; the quaint old forms -- elections, parliaments, Supreme Courts and all the rest -- will remain. The underlying substance will be a new kind of non-violent totalitarianism. All the traditional names, all the hallowed slogans will remain exactly what they were in the good old days. Democracy and freedom will be the theme of every broadcast and editorial [...]. **Meanwhile the ruling oligarchy and its highly trained elite of soldiers, policemen, thought-manufacturers and**

---

[83] The market is the sum total of all voluntary economic transactions among the eight billion people on the planet.

mind-manipulators will quietly run the show as they see fit."

—Aldous Huxley, *Brave New World Revisited* (1958) (Emphasis added)

MEASURING LEGITIMATE GOVERNMENT VIOLENCE

A small percentage of government gun violence may be related to the small number of things government does that could be justified by the libertarian theory of the Declaration of Independence, when Lockean government is actually protecting individual rights. Jefferson further refined the concept in his First Inaugural Address: "a wise and frugal Government, which *shall restrain men from injuring one another,* shall leave them otherwise free to regulate their own pursuits of industry and improvement, and shall not take from the mouth of labor the bread it has earned. This is the sum of good government . . . " (Emphasis added)

Libertarians may argue about the best mechanism to enforce rights, but we all agree in theory that people may delegate their natural right of self-defense to others and that delegation is legitimate. So, for our purposes, we may *exclude* from our current calculation of government violence any actual measures, however clumsy or ineffective, that vindicate individual rights. For example, when a man is getting mugged and the police come to his rescue and arrest the mugger; then when a court tries the man and sentences the man and incarcerates him for some period of time; although we can argue and we do about whether that is the most efficient or just way of deterring crime, we cannot deny some legitimacy to the activity and can concede that that particular use of government force was justified as a form of delegated self-defense under Lockean principles. Also, when government repels an invasion or attack from another country or from terrorists, we can concede for our present purposes that such force is being legitimately used for defending individual rights.

So, the question is, out of the whole massive quantity of current government force, what approximate percentage is devoted to the pure defense of individuals against aggressive force from others? This can only be an estimate, but we *must* make a reasonable estimate to resolve the debate over the right to bear arms versus gun control. Fortunately, we did once have a government that was much more limited than the colossus we suffer under today and we know roughly what percent of national income it consumed. If we compare that figure to current expenditures, we begin to develop a method of calculation.

Around 1900, total government spending was less than ten percent of GDP but has risen to almost 40 percent today.[84] For example, public social spending rose from less than one percent in 1880 to about 20% today.[85] And yet, America was no pure libertarian republic in 1900. By then, there was compulsory schooling in almost every state

---

[84]   https://taxfoundation.org/data/all/state/growth-government-spending-twentieth-century;
https://www.statista.com/statistics/268356/ratio-of-government-expenditure-to-gross-domestic-product-gdp-in-the-united-states/
[85] *Source:* ourworldindata.org

involving massive expenditures and several federal programs that violated Jeffersonian limited government principles such as the Department of Agriculture. America started to fight imperialistic foreign wars. Money was wasted on canals that would soon be obsolete and railroads that were built in the wrong places for political reasons.[86] We can safely state that no more than half of 1900 spending was for pure libertarian self-defense, if that. Since total spending is now about 40% of GDP and legitimate spending was no more than 5%, we can conclude that at best only a small fraction of current spending is even arguably legitimate.

We can see why by examining current government spending at all levels of government. Federal, state and local government spending is about $10.5 trillion. [87] USGovernmentSpending.com breaks down spending as follows: defense—$1.3 trillion; protection—$367 billion; and general government—$251 billion. The rest is basically transfer payments and "education" and other matters not within the narrow scope of the Lockean minimal state which is limited to exercising the people's delegated power of self-defense. What is described as "defense" spending is a misnomer. Very little of the United States Defense budget involves actual defense as the United States proper has not been invaded by a foreign army since 1812 and is highly unlikely to be invaded in the near future. The United States passed from republic to empire around the time of the Spanish-American War and its current military budget largely pays for a global military empire with 750 bases

---

[86] Thomas DiLorenzo, *How Capitalism Saved America* (2005).
[87] USGovernmentspending.com.

around the world. Its military budget is two times the size of its main rivals, Russia and China, combined.[88]

The Founders were suspicious of large standing armies and favored a citizen militia instead. If the bloated military budget was reduced to $432 billion, then true defense spending, protection and general government spending would constitute about ten percent of current spending. That is a generous estimate as many of the elements of "protection" and "general government" such as the war on drugs and war on guns are beyond the scope of the classical liberal minimal state. Thus, our estimate that no more than *ten percent* of current spending and government activity is legitimate is a conservative one.

The overwhelming portion of total government spending involves matters not only not within the purview of a classical liberal natural rights-protecting republic, but involves programs that contradict and violate that function. These programs include all transfer payments, all compulsory and/or tax supported education, socialized medicine, the regulatory[89] state and the global military empire. Even assuming, for the sake of argument, that taxation is justified to pay for the function of a minimal state with courts, police, prisons and national defense,[90] it is *not* justified for any other functions, and indeed, must be

---

[88] Sipri.org.

[89] "Regulation" is a propaganda term. Its actual meaning is either a tax on non-monetary wealth or the imposition of government coercion on someone engaging in intrinsically benign behavior.

[90] *Contra*, Rothbard, *Ethics of Liberty* (1982); Ayn Rand, "Ayn Rand on Tax Day," *The Economist* (April 15, 2011).

deemed violent extortion, robbery and theft. Calvin Coolidge would have agreed. He stated, "Collecting more taxes than is absolutely necessary is legalized robbery." The great Jeffersonian Grover Cleveland expressed a similar sentiment:

> "When more of the people's sustenance is exacted through the form of taxation than is necessary to meet the just obligations of government and expenses of its economical administration, such exaction becomes ruthless extortion and a violation of the fundamental principles of free government."[91]

Spending is not the only means of estimating government force. Since 1900, the modern regulatory state that controls almost every aspect of our daily lives and always backed up by an implied threat of government gun violence has been installed. A war on drugs, one of the most violent and intrusive government policies, leading as it does to the arrest of millions and the incarceration of hundreds of thousands for imaginary crimes, was commenced. A bit later, its cousin, the war on guns, was rolled out. Both wars against private property[92] and liberty work together to provide the motive for a huge number of traffic stops, roadblocks and stop and frisks on the street. The war on

---

[91] https://fee.org/articles/clinton-versus-cleveland-and-coolidge-on-taxes/

[92] Thomas Szasz, *Our Right to Drugs: The Case for a Free Market* (1992).

guns is likewise responsible for a huge number of arrests and incarcerations of peaceful people violating no one's natural rights.

The classical liberal view of the Founders was brilliantly expressed in 1798 by Supreme Court Justice Samuel Chase, a signer of the Declaration of Independence, in an opinion that would be considered heresy today:

> "The people of the United States erected their constitutions, or forms of government, to establish justice, to promote the general welfare, to secure the blessings of liberty, *and to protect their persons and property from violence.* The purposes for which men enter into society will determine the nature and terms of the social compact, and as they are the foundation of the legislative power, they will decide what are the proper objects of it. The nature and ends of legislative power will limit the exercise of it. This fundamental principle flows from the very nature of our free republican governments that no man should be compelled to do what the laws do not require nor to refrain from acts which the laws permit. *There are acts which the federal or state legislature cannot do without exceeding their authority. There are certain vital principles in our free republican governments which will determine and overrule an apparent and flagrant abuse of legislative power, as to authorize manifest injustice by positive law or to take away that security for personal liberty or private property for the protection whereof . . . the*

government was established. An act of the legislature (for I cannot call it a law) contrary to the great first principles of the social compact cannot be considered a rightful exercise of legislative authority. The obligation of a law in governments established on express compact and on republican principles must be determined by the nature of the power on which it is founded.

"A few instances will suffice to explain what I mean. A law that punished a citizen for an innocent action, or in other words for an act which when done was in violation of no existing law; a law that destroys or impairs the lawful private contracts of citizens; a law that makes a man a judge in his own cause, or a law that takes property from A. and gives it to B. It is against all reason and justice for a people to entrust a legislature with such powers, and therefore it cannot be presumed that it has done it. The genius, the nature, and the spirit of our state governments amount to a prohibition of such acts of legislation, and the general principles of law and reason forbid them. The legislature may enjoin, permit, forbid, and punish; It may declare new crimes and establish rules of conduct for all its citizens in future cases; it may command what is right and prohibit what is wrong, but it cannot change innocence into guilt or punish innocence as a crime or violate the right of an antecedent lawful private contract or the right of private property. To maintain that our federal or state legislature possesses such powers if it had not been expressly restrained would, in my opinion, be a political heresy altogether inadmissible in our free republican governments."[93]

The views of Chase, Coolidge and Cleveland may seem quaint if not antiquated. The modern, progressive view is to the contrary. Forget all that old libertarian *republican*[94] theory; we are an unlimited *democracy* now and the government can do whatever it damn well pleases since majority rules. However, where is the *argument* that democracy, a deeply flawed collective decision-making technology, overrides *all* prior understandings of morality, right and wrong, natural law and natural human rights? There is no such argument. As libertarian philosopher David Gordon writes:

> "Though it is easy to characterize democracy, recent political theory has been marked by a conspicuous omission. Virtually no argument is ever offered to support the desirability of representative democracy, and the little that is available seems distressingly weak. Why ought democracy to be either instituted or promoted, let alone exported, as a recent book by Joshua

---

[93] *Calder v. Bull*, 3 U.S. 386 (1798).

[94] By "republican," I mean a government exercising limited powers delegated to them by the people and who are accountable to the people in regular elections.

> Muravchik (*Exporting Democracy*) advocates? One would think that as important a question as that of the best political system would have generated an enormous literature. In point of fact, most writing on the subject simply takes for granted the desirability of democracy and inquires how existing democracies may be improved. The issue of whether democracy is a 'good thing' is not thought worth raising."[95]

This is why my argument may not be easily dismissed. Sacred progressive democracy *does*, as a matter of observable empirical fact, inflict violent harm on individuals and this *does* require a logical or moral justification which, as Dr. Gordon perceptively notes, has not been forthcoming! Libertarians await your argument with bated breath. Please tweet it to me @JimOstrowski so I can be bowled over by your brilliance in real time. In the meantime, I will side with Augustine, Aquinas ("an unjust law is no law at all.") Locke, Jefferson, Chase, Cleveland, Coolidge, A. Rand and Robert Nozick: no more than the minimal state is morally or practically justifiable. *All the surplusage is essentially criminal violence.* Nozick said it well:

> "Individuals have rights, and there are things no person or group may do to them (without violating their rights). . . . [A] minimal state, limited to the narrow functions of protection

---

[95] What's the Argument for Democracy? <u>LewRockwell.com</u> (Dec. 29, 2016)

against force, theft, fraud, enforcement of contracts, and so on, is justified . . . any more extensive state will violate persons' rights not to be forced to do certain things, and is unjustified. . . ."[96]

Saint Augustine expressed a similar sentiment 1500 years earlier:

"Justice being taken away, then, what are kingdoms but great robberies? For what are robberies themselves, but little kingdoms? The band itself is made up of men; it is ruled by the authority of a prince, it is knit together by the pact of the confederacy; the booty is divided by the law agreed on. If, by the admittance of abandoned men, this evil increases to such a degree that it holds places, fixes abodes, takes possession of cities, and subdues peoples, it assumes the more plainly the name of a kingdom, because the reality is now manifestly conferred on it, not by the removal of covetousness, but by the addition of impunity. Indeed, that was an apt and true reply which was given to Alexander the Great by a pirate who had been seized. For when that king had asked the man what he meant by keeping hostile possession of the sea, he answered with bold pride, 'What thou

---

[96] *Anarchy, State and Utopia* (1974), p. ix.

meanest by seizing the whole earth; but because I do it with a petty ship, I am called a robber, whilst thou who dost it with a great fleet art styled emperor.'"[97]

The core ideology of the Founders was libertarian-republican natural rights theory. Since the notion of a stateless society was not in currency until William Godwin's book *Enquiry Concerning Political Justice and its Influence on Morals and Happiness,* published in 1793 and Gustave Molinari's work *The Production of Security* in 1849, the Founders were not anarchists but favored a *minimal* government restricted to protecting individual natural rights. Nevertheless they understood that government, as Thomas Paine wrote in *Common Sense,* ". . . even in its best state, is but a necessary evil; in its worst state an intolerable one: for when we suffer, or are exposed to the same miseries BY A GOVERNMENT, which we might expect in a country WITHOUT GOVERNMENT, our calamity is heightened by reflecting that we furnish the means by which we suffer." They believed that any amount of government beyond that required to fulfill its core function of defense was tyrannical in nature. Thus, the approach and methodology of this book is consistent with the core philosophy of the Founding.

The modern, left-progressive, regulatory, imperialistic, paternalistic, welfare-warfare state is obviously far beyond the minimal state envisioned by the Founders. It is an unnecessary evil that has never been justified. Rather, the

---

[97] *City of God* Book IV Chapter 4.

new model emerged with an intellectual coup d'etat during the Progressive Era and began to drastically expand government around 1913-14. [98] Not only has the progressive state never been justified; it never fulfilled its promises either. This was the subject of my book *Progressivism: A Primer.* In that book, the failures of progressive policy wherever it was tried are explained in detail. Thus, even if morally justified, it has been a practical disaster.

DEMOCRATIC VIOLENCE IS
STILL VIOLENCE!

Granted, there is no valid argument for pure, unlimited, majoritarian democracy as a fancy form of ethical nihilism: whatever some ephemeral and manipulated electorate votes for is beyond any moral reproach. Even if this was true, it nevertheless remains the case that democratic government inflicts *violence* against individuals and this violence is *real* and has *real* economic costs and hence *must* be counted in any rational calculus of societal violence and in any definition of or calculation of societal peace! This conclusion is buttressed by the World Health Organization's definition of violence, which, notably does not obviously exclude government violence from its ambit:

> "the intentional use of physical force or
> power, threatened or actual, against oneself,

---

[98] Murray Rothbard, *The Progressive Era* (2017).

another person, or against a group or community that either results in or has a high likelihood of resulting in injury, death, psychological harm, maldevelopment or deprivation."[99]

Economist Murray Rothbard explained the *economic* harm done by government gun violence:

"Coercive intervention . . . signifies per se that the individual or individuals coerced would not have done what they are now doing were it not for the intervention. The individual who is coerced into saying or not saying something or into making or not making an exchange with the intervener or with someone else is having his actions changed by a threat of violence. The coerced individual loses in utility as a result of the intervention, for his action has been changed by its impact. Any intervention, whether it be autistic, binary, or triangular, causes the subjects to lose in utility. . . . All instances of intervention, then, in contrast to the free market, are cases in which one set of men gains at the expense of other men. In binary intervention, the gains and losses are 'tangible' in the form of exchangeable goods

---

[99]   https://www.who.int/groups/violence-prevention-alliance/approach

and services; in other types of intervention, the gains are nonexchangeable satisfactions, and the loss consists in being coerced into less satisfying types of activity (if not positively painful ones)."[100]

Elsewhere, Rothbard explains:

"Directly, coercion benefits one party only at the expense of others. Coerced exchange is a system of exploitation of man by man, in contrast to the free market, which is a system of cooperative exchanges in the exploitation of nature alone. And not only does coerced exchange mean that some live at the expense of others, but, indirectly, as we have just observed, coercion leads only to further problems: it is inefficient and chaotic, it cripples production, and it leads to cumulative and unforeseen difficulties. Seemingly orderly, coercion is not only exploitative; it is also profoundly disorderly."[101]

Thus, I have proven in several different ways that aggressive government violence, even *democratic* government violence is still destructive violence by any rational definition. The essence of violence is the negation

---

[100] *Power and Market, supra* at 13-14.

[101] *Man, Economy and State* (1962), p. 880.

of individual choice or liberty. It substitutes the perpetrator's judgment for the victim's and thus negates the victim's rational mind, the essence of their humanity, in that range of action subject to the violence. Negation of the individual mind is the unifying theme of all forms of violence.[102] Indeed, that is its precise purpose. As Ayn Rand wrote, "A gun is not an argument." *Government violence is therefore appropriately factored into our rankings of countries.* By refusing to *ignore* some kinds of violence, this book actually fulfills the promise made by the Gun Violence Archive[103] and the World Health Organization[104] to calculate societal violence in an empirical and scientific manner.

SUMMARY

In this chapter, I have laid the foundation for a cautious estimate that, when you combine the enormous increases in spending, in coercive regulations of peaceful people and the arrest and prosecution of those accused of imaginary crimes, as well as the creation of an enormous global military empire that almost exclusively fights aggressive, not defensive wars, that no more than *ten percent* of current government activity can be justified on pure libertarian grounds and it is probably much less. Thus, at least 90 percent of current government force is *illegitimate*

---

[102] This is a major theme of Ayn Rand's fiction and non-fiction works.

[103] https://www.gunviolencearchive.org/methodology

[104] https://www.who.int/groups/violence-prevention-alliance/approach

and essentially in the same category as private sector violence (crime) and thus may be compared with the degree of such violence for purposes of this debate.

Since criminals commit a mere 285,000 gun crimes each year and the government probably commits trillions of acts of violence, even if we *deduct* legitimate delegated self-defense and true national defense activities, I have proven that government gun violence far exceeds that committed by criminals. We can safely conclude that illegitimate government violence constitutes *far more than 99 percent* of all gun violence in the United States.

Thus, in this chapter, I have proven that:

1. The government is by far the leading cause of gun violence in our society.

2. At least ninety percent of this violence cannot be justified by the natural rights libertarian republican theory of the Declaration of Independence, America's founding document.

3. Even with respect to the relatively tiny number of private sector gun crimes, the overwhelming percentage of these are directly or indirectly the result of failed government policies and the government, despite arrogating to itself vast powers and funding, failed to stop these crimes. Indeed, by violating the

victims' right to bear arms, the government effectively disarmed many of the victims and helped facilitate many of these crimes.

More gun control will vastly increase illegitimate government gun violence directly while indirectly encouraging further government growth by centralizing ever more power in the government.

Thus, a leading premise of the gun control movement, that gun violence in America is primarily committed by private individuals and can be cured by giving the government even more power, has been destroyed forever.

3. The United States is *Not* an Unusually Violent Country

This chapter will address the other leading premise of the gun control movement, that the United States is an unusually violent country because of widespread civilian gun ownership. This too is utter nonsense. The gun controllers make their case by manipulating statistics and leaving out the most important statistics.

There are in fact at least *five* separate measures of violence in any society, yet they only address *one* of them: crime. Even here, they mix in statistics about suicides to inflate the numbers and mislead the public. And, in comparison with other countries that have fewer guns, they do not talk about violent crime per se but only crimes committed *with a firearm*. In *The Second Amendment Works,* I explained why suicide is a separate and distinct issue from other forms of violence. While as a Catholic and someone who aspires to be a humanitarian, I view suicide as a tragic event, it is absurd to equate one person's choice to take his own life with another person's choice to take the life of another. In truth, suicide is not primarily a political problem at all. Politics deals with the proper interrelationships of persons in society; suicide in sharp contrast involves a personal decision concerning whether to continue living. Regardless of what third parties wish, each individual must in the end choose to continue living or not.

It should be noted that the gun control movement's concern about suicide seems disingenuous. Just as they rarely if ever concern themselves with the actual underlying causes of *crime*, neither do they express much interest in the underlying causes of *suicide*. Their only real concern seems to be disarming individuals and thereby facilitating endless government growth.

CRIME

If we take international statistics about the most reliably measured crime, homicide, where does the United States actually rank?[105] Not first or in the top ten but 76th.[106] This is not a terrible ranking for a large, diverse country with an open southern border and a raging drug war started by the government itself.

So, if we exclude suicides and include homicide *by all methods*, the United States is not particularly violent given its unique nature which renders comparisons to other countries

---

[105] It should be noted that the ranking of the rate of homicides in the United States is probably overstated because of a large degree of underreporting of the same crime internationally. See, R. Kleinfeld, Reducing Violent Deaths, Everywhere: Why the Data Must Improve," carnegieendowment.org (Feb. 2, 2017); R. McMaken, "With Few Gun Laws, New Hampshire is Safer Than Canada," mises.org (Dec. 15, 2015) ("One is likely to find suspiciously low homicide rates in many authoritarian countries. . . ")

[106] https://www.datapandas.org/ranking/violent-crime-rates-by-country#methodology; United Nations Office on Drugs and Crime; (Using numbers from 2019 as representing a typical year. Note that the U. S. murder rate rose during the Lockdown years and George Floyd riots and was recently reported to be lowering. However, current comparable data is not yet available.)

subject to caution. Further, the homicide rate is particularly high in neighborhoods destroyed by failed progressive and Great Society programs,[107] rendering the vast bulk of the rest of the country about as safe as the tiny monocultural countries whose crimes statistics the gun controllers love to cite. For example, the crime rate in New Hampshire is comparable to much of Europe even though citizens there are well armed and have constitutional carry.[108] In other words, the homicide rate in *England* is not far off from the homicide rate in *New England.* Likewise, the crime rate in Ireland is not too different from the crime rate in Irish neighborhoods in the United States like the one I grew up in, South Buffalo, where violent crime was virtually unheard of.

So much for their main propaganda point. Yet, their distortion of this one statistical category does not even begin to capture the flaws in their propaganda. They completely ignore the four *other* major categories of violence.

GOVERNMENT VIOLENCE

In any society, as shown in Chapter 2, *the government* is the main cause of illegitimate violence, that is, not justified by self-defense. The gun controllers completely ignore this category of violence, in fact, they want to vastly increase government gun violence. Yet, we have already seen how gigantic this factor is. The question is, can we compare this

---

[107] See, James Ostrowski, *Progressive Big Government's War on Black People (1865-2021)* Kindle Edition (2021).
[108] R. McMaken, "With Few Gun Laws, New Hampshire is Safer Than Canada," mises.org (Dec. 15, 2015).

type of violence between and among countries? To crunch these kinds of numbers for 165 countries and then compare them would be almost impossible, however, after puzzling over this conundrum, I realized there *is* a way to measure government violence *indirectly* by reference to the Human Freedom Index created by the Cato and Fraser Institutes. [109] They have created an elaborate ranking of which countries have the least and most freedom and we can infer that those with the most freedom have the *least* illegitimate government violence basically by definition. They rank the largest 165 countries in the world that constitute about 99 percent of the world's population. Every variable used by the Human Freedom Index measures how much individual freedom is destroyed by government coercion or violence. Therefore, their measurement of freedom provides a measurement of the opposite side of the coin: government violence.

Sadly, the United States freedom ranking has declined since Barack Obama was president and through the subsequent lockdowns and free spending by Donald Trump and Joe Biden and is now ranked somewhat lower than in the past. [110] Nevertheless, the United States still has a relatively high ranking in an unfree world. Out of 165 countries ranked, the United States is ranked 17th best. However, this ranking is a bit misleading as the only large country ranked above the United States is Japan, an

---

[109] Cato.org/human-freedom-index/2023. The Index does not rank Afghanistan, by all accounts an extremely violent country.

[110] https://www.cato.org/blog/us-ranks-17-hong-kong-plummets-argentina-decline-new-human-freedom-index

island and historically idiosyncratic monocultural United States protectorate.[111] There are 13 relatively small countries in *Europe* or that are *European* in culture and monocultural, e.g., Latvia and Iceland. These include six islands.[112] The only other country ranked higher than the United States is Taiwan, a small, monocultural United States protectorate and island. Also, the difference in rank between No. 1, well-armed Switzerland, at 9.01, is not drastically above the United States rating of 8.39.

As I noted in my book, *The Second Amendment Works,* it is difficult to find a country similar to the United States in size, population, diversity and open borders, yet, the gun control movement never hesitates to make such unwarranted comparisons. The United States southern border is wide open to travelers from about 20 "undeveloped" Latin American countries. I find it more useful to compare the United States to several other countries that *are* comparable in at least size and population. These include India, China, Russia, Brazil and Indonesia. The United States compares quite favorably to these other large states. Brazil ranks 73rd, Indonesia 92nd, India 109th, Russia 121st and China, a critic of our right to bear arms and our leading economic rival, which has notoriously few guns and which mowed down

---

[111] See *Death by Gun Control*, Chapter 21. It turns out that Japan has more liberty on paper than in reality.

[112] In ranking countries by their degree of violence, islands would seem to have a natural advantage as they share no borders with other countries. They have no border disputes by definition, a major cause of conflict. They have a natural protective barrier to invasion and have less concern about violent criminals crossing their borders on foot.

hundreds, if not thousands of protestors at Tiananmen Square,[113] is ranked a pathetic 149th. These low freedom rankings indicate that these governments inflict a massive amount of government gun violence upon their citizens.

Brazil is by all accounts a very violent country while Russia and China are well-known authoritarian regimes with sordid recent histories. [114] Indonesia, however, is an interesting case with low levels of gun ownership and apparently low levels of homicide. However, their Travel Advisory is more revealing:

"Exercise increased caution in Indonesia due to terrorism and natural disasters. Do Not travel to: The provinces of Central Papua (Papua Tengah) and Highland Papua (Papua Pegunungan) due to civil unrest.

Terrorists continue plotting possible attacks in Indonesia. Terrorists may attack with little or no warning, targeting police stations, places of worship, hotels, bars, nightclubs, markets/shopping malls, and restaurants. . . . Demonstrations occur frequently and have the potential to become violent. Avoid demonstrations and crowds. If you decide to travel to Indonesia: Monitor local media for breaking events and be prepared to adjust your plans. . . . Be aware of your personal safety and

---

[113]   https://www.amnesty.org.uk/china-1989-tiananmen-square-protests-demonstration-massacre

[114] Rachel Kleinfeld, *supra,* points out that China's statistics on internal violence are not reliable.

security at all times. Central Papua and Highland Papua– Level 4: Do Not Travel In Central Papua and Highland Papua, violent demonstrations and conflict could result in injury or death to U.S. citizens. Avoid demonstrations and crowds. Armed separatists may kidnap foreign nationals."

India's travel advisory is also disturbing:

"Exercise increased caution in India due to crime and terrorism.

"Do not travel to:

"The union territory of Jammu and Kashmir (except the eastern Ladakh region and its capital, Leh) due to terrorism and civil unrest. Within 10 km of the India-Pakistan border due to the potential for armed conflict.
Country Summary: Indian authorities report rape is one of the fastest growing crimes in India. Violent crime, such as sexual assault, has occurred at tourist sites and in other locations. Terrorists may attack with little or no warning, targeting tourist locations, transportation hubs, markets/shopping malls, and government facilities. . . .
If you decide to travel to India:
Do not travel alone, particularly if you are a woman. Visit our website for Women Travelers.

Review your personal security plans and remain alert to your surroundings."[115]

Thus, even though we have slipped, the United States, the country with by far the most guns per capita on the planet, measures up quite well in government gun violence when compared to other large countries.

Given that government violence is the single most important contributor to violence in any society, I conclude that this factor should be given the greatest weight among the five factors, at least 50 percent. And, not to get ahead of ourselves, this factor will weigh heavily against the myth of the United States as an unusually violent country.

TERRORISM

The third of the five factors I see as critical in ranking countries by their level of violence is *terrorism*.

This factor is entirely ignored by gun controllers. Indeed, they have been known to studiously *ignore* foreign mass shootings as somehow irrelevant to the gun control debate (e.g., Israel, October 7, 2023 and Russia, March 23, 2024). Yet, terrorism must be evaluated to get a complete picture of the relative degree of violence *inside* countries. You might think that the United States would lead the world in terror attacks as it is by far the most interventionist country in the world and has porous borders and a diverse population. Yet, it is *not* a leader in terrorist

---

[115] https://travel.state.gov/content/travel/en/traveladvisori es/traveladvisories/india-travel-advisory.html

attacks. It ranks only 30th in the most recent Global Terrorism Index.[116]

Terrorism results in relatively few actual deaths but has an impact beyond the immediate victims as it is intended to instill fear throughout society. Though resulting in relatively few casualties, terrorism punches above its statistical weight by inflicting substantial psychological harm on societies, by interjecting fear and violence into political decision-making and by encouraging often counterproductive policy responses such as the Patriot Act and the American invasion of Iraq in 2003. Terrorism is an engine of government growth. That said, I believe this factor is entitled to a five percent weight in arriving at a calculation of a country's overall level of violence.

WAR CASUALTIES

The fourth factor is also ignored by the gun controllers: *war casualties* inside a country. They like to claim that the United States is unusually violent compared to other countries but completely ignore the fact that many countries have had devastating wars *on their soil* for decades and *currently* and the United States has not. War casualties, whether in classic interstate wars or civil wars, obviously must be counted in evaluating any country's level of violence. War carries with it many other evils not subject to easy calculus. Chief among those evils is the inevitable abuse of women in the form of mass rape as a weapon of war. American women

---

[116] https://www.visionofhumanity.org/maps/global-terrorism-index/#/

(citizens) have been largely spared this war crime and atrocity except for the Civil War. Based on a confirmed number of 450 court-martials for rape against white and black Southern women, we can safely assume that there were thousands of such rapes with most going unreported and unpunished.[117] It *can* happen here, because it *has* happened here.

Following their legendary methodology of cherry-picking data and ignoring all contrary evidence and data, gun controllers studiously ignore all the countries in the world that have ongoing conflicts *and* low gun ownership and/or strict gun laws, usually both. See, Table No. 4.

---

[117] Julie Beck, "Gender, Race, and Rape During the Civil War," *The Atlantic* (Feb. 20, 2014); see also, Thomas DiLorenzo, *The Real Lincoln: A New Look at Abraham Lincoln, His Agenda, and an Unnecessary War* (2003), p. 188.

Table No. 4.

Many Countries Without an Armed Population Are Violent and Unstable

Countries with ongoing civil war or major internal conflict or unrest *Sources:* WorldPopulation Review.com; Wikipedia; Statista.com; Human Rights Watch; Google News	Guns per 100 people (U. S. = 120.5) *Source:* Wikipedia	Number of times Everytown.org or Giffords.org touted the benefits of gun control in these countries *Sources:* Google and a search of their websites
Afghanistan	12.5	0
Burkina Faso	0.9	0
Burundi	2.0	0
Colombia	10.1	0
Central African Republic	1.8	0
DR Congo	1.2	0

Eritrea	0.4	0
Ethiopia	0.4	0
Iraq	19.6	0
Mali	1.1	0
Mexico	12.9	0 (Giffords and Everytown blame the U. S. for the failure of Mexico's gun laws.)
Myanmar	1.6	0
Nigeria	3.2	0
Rwanda	0.5	0
Somalia	12.4	0
South Sudan	9.6	0
Sudan	6.6	0
Syria	8.2	0
Venezuela	18.5	0
Yemen	52.8	0
Average	8.8	NA
Median	4.9	NA

The causal connection between war and peace and a well-armed civilian population is explored in *The Second Amendment Works*. I noted for example that the militia was a significant factor in resisting the last invasion of America in 1812. I also noted that Japan never launched a land invasion during World War II, possibly because of the fear of "an

American with a rifle behind every blade of grass." True, that quote is probably fabricated but the logic behind it is not. No army wants to fight another standing army and then a guerrilla war. A well-armed civilian population *is* a deterrent to foreign invasion. This may explain why no American state has been invaded since the War of 1812 (not counting the Civil War.) The last war casualty on American soil was in World War II when a woman was killed by a rigged Japanese explosive balloon.[118]

The extremely low rate of contemporary combat or civil war deaths in the United States must be counted in determining an overall violence score for this country. There are currently anywhere from 27-40 armed conflicts raging in the world, depending on definitions, but *none* are in the United States I propose to assign a relative weight of 15% to this factor. Because of the infrequency of the incidents that produce these casualties, using current statistics does not capture the full reality of such violence. A longer period of measurement is called for to avoid giving too much weight to infrequent and unusual events. Using the period from 1950 through the present approximates the average human life span on the planet. In that way, we are measuring events that actually affected many people still alive today. We also conveniently avoid factoring in the colossal tragedy of World War II lest it skew the numbers. However horrendous that event was, it has not been repeated and it was not replicated previously even by World War I. Although World War I was also a human catastrophe that continues to exert a negative influence on current

---

[118]   https://time.com/6276685/japanese-balloon-bomb-history-world-war-ii/

events, it is even more remote than World War II and its death count was far lower than World War II (18 million to 70 million).[119]

Given that time frame, there was no single authoritative source for comparative statistics on war casualties. Rather, the author created a ranking of countries from worst to best based on a variety of sources. The results are contained in Table No. 5. The table is based on the *recency of the war* and the *number of deaths*. All countries with zero war casualties are ranked as tied for "last" place. For purposes of the Global Violence Index rolled out in Chapter 4, the order of countries is reversed.

---

[119] borgenproject.org/top-12-deadliest-wars-in-history/

Table No. 5

War Casualties in Country
Since 1950

Compiled by the Author from a variety of sources.

Sources: Uppsala Conflict Data Program, Wikipedia, Polynational War Memorial, Wars and Casualties of the 20th and 21st Centuries (Piero Scaruffi)

Note: estimates of fatalities from ongoing conflicts is likely to be significantly underestimated.

Ongoing Conflicts

1. SYRIA 2011-2024, 390,512
2. AFGHANISTAN, 1989-2024, 304,529
3. ETHIOPIA 1989-2024, 287,666
4. IRAQ, 2003-2024, 106,858
5. MEXICO, 2005-2024, 95,227
6. UKRAINE, 2014-2024, 90,265
7. SUDAN 1989-2024, 75,946
8. YEMEN, 2011-2024, 65,302
9. SOMALIA, 1989-2024, 55,223
10. DR CONGO, 1993-2024, 51,134
11. NIGERIA, 1989-2024, 49,001
12. INDIA, 1989-2024, 46,991
13. PAKISTAN, 2003-2024, 39,604
14. TURKEY, 1989-2024, 30,173

15. COLOMBIA, 1989-2024, 27,512
16. RUSSIA, 1989-2024, 22,798
17. PHILLIPPINES, 1989-2024, 19,586
18. MYANMAR/BURMA, 2021-2024, 17,355
19. BURUNDI, 1989-2024, 15,324
20. LIBYA, 2011-2024, 13,698
21. AZERBAIJAN, 1990-2024, 13,240
22. BURKINA FASO, 2015-2024, 10,000
23. MALI, 1989-2024, 9,399
24. ISRAEL, 1989-2024, 8,317
25. CHAD, 1989-2024, 8012
26. MOZAMBIQUE, 2017-2024, 7019
27. CENTRAL AFRICAN REPUBLIC, 2001-2024, 6,881
28. SOUTH SUDAN, 2011-2024, 5,591
29. LEBANON, 1989-2024, 5,675
30. CAMEROON, 2013-2024, 5554
31. KENYA, 1989-2024, 5078
32. BURKINA FASO, 2018-2024, 4283
33. THAILAND, 2004-2024, 2189
34. NIGER, 1989-2024, 1947
35. IRAN, 1990-2024, 1908
36. BANGLADESH, 1989-2024, 823
37. PAPUA NEW GUINEA, 1989-2024, 658
38. HAITI, 1989-2024, 638
39. ARMENIA, 1991-2024, 363
40. VENEZUELA, 1989-2024, 351
41. TUNISIA, 2001-2024, 346

42. HONDURAS, 1998-2024, 255

21ST CENTURY

43. SRI LANKA, 1989-2010, 61,878
44. ANGOLA, 1989-2002, 30,730
45. ALGERIA, 1992-2018, 19,499
46. UGANDA 1989-2010, 12,009
47. NEPAL, 1998-2006, 9,954
48. INDONESIA, 1990-2006, 6328
49. LIBERIA, 1990-2004, 6074
50. EGYPT, 1992-2021, 4950
51. SENEGAL, 1989-2012, 1737
52. GUINEA, 1996-2021, 851
53. GEORGIA, 2007-2009, 621

1976-2000

54. CAMBODIA, 1979-1998, 87,499
55. EL SALVADOR, 1979-1991, 51,809
56. BOSNIA, 1992-1995, 49,835
57. GUATEMALA 1965-1995—45,418
58. NICARAUGUA, 1978-1990, 39,965
59. SIERRA LEONE, 1991-2000, 20,157
60. TAJIKISTAN, 1991-1999, 9334
61. RWANDA, 1990-1994, 7,963
62. SERBIA, 1991-2000, 7,774
63. PERU, 1989-2000, 6987

64. SOUTH AFRICA, 1989-1998, 4902
65. ALBANIA, 1997, 2000
66. CROATIA, 1992-1995, 1313
67. PANAMA, 1989, 920
68. ROMANIA, 1989, 909

1950-1975

69. VIETNAM 1955-1964—164,923; 1965-1975—
    2,048,050
70. CHINA 1959, 87,000
71. LAOS, 1959-1973, 21,500
72. MALAYSIA, 1948-57, 10,845
73. CYPRUS, 1974, 5000
74. DOMINICAN REPUBLIC, 1965, 4027
75. HUNGARY, 1956, 3171
76. CHILE, 1973, 2095
77. CUBA, 1953-61, 1205
78. TAIWAN, 1954-58, 1007
79. BOLIVIA, 1952, 1000
80. ALL OTHER COUNTRIES TIED FOR LAST.

DEMOCIDE

Finally, there is yet another cause of violence that gun controllers choose to ignore in their calculations about the relative level of violence in the United States. Throughout history, governments and states and regimes have *murdered* huge numbers of their own non-combatant citizens or subjects. R. J. Rummel (1932-2014) called this "democide"[120] and devoted his life to chronicling ancient, historical and modern democides and estimating the number of victims in each country in each era. In the last 100 years, there were massive waves of democide, most notably in Germany, the Soviet Union, Communist China, and Cambodia. Surely, the avoidance of democide and its inevitable concomitant, mass rape, inside the United States is a crucial factor in determining its level of violence in comparison to other countries. I propose that ten percent of the formula for measuring peace and violence should be attributed to the historical level of democide in each country. Like war casualties, democides are relatively rare and thus we must reach back into history for meaningful statistics. As with war, however, if we reach too far back, we risk giving undue weight to events whose contemporary relevance has diminished. Again, I propose to use 1950 to the present as a demarcation line as approximating a period of time matching the average human life span.

Given that timeline, there wasn't a single authoritative source for measuring democide and ranking countries by their degree of democide. I therefore had to rank countries using a variety of sources. These sources include R. J. Rummel's research which pertains exclusively to the period from 1950 through 2000. I also rely heavily on the "Early Warning Project," indeed, I retain their ranking of countries which is based on a sophisticated current risk assessment of

---

[120] Now often called "one-sided killing."

democide.[121] However, I disagree with the Early Warning Project insofar as they provide a risk assessment of countries that do not appear to have had any mass killings on their lands since 1950. Notably, these countries include the United States, Canada and Switzerland. Since I am basing my ranking primarily on actual mass killings in that country, my list excludes all such countries for which there is no evidence of democide since 1950 and hence all such countries are listed as tied for "last place" in the democide rankings in Table No. 6. In the Global Violence Index introduced in Chapter 4, the column evaluating democide is based on Table No. 6 except that the order of countries is reversed.

Table No. 6

Democide List

Ranked by the Early Warning Project

Risk of Current Democide

1.	AFGHANISTAN, 6.5%
2.	PAKISTAN, 6.1%
3.	YEMEN, 5.9%

---

[121]   EarlyWarningProject.ushmm.org   (United States Holocaust Memorial Museum). My whole approach to statistics in this book is to base them on pre-existing credible sources whenever possible so as to minimize the impression that I have manipulated statistics myself to advance the thesis of this book.

4.   SUDAN, 5.7%
5.   INDIA, 5.3%
6.   ETHIOPIA, 5.1%
7.   GUINEA, 4.5%
8.   SOMALIA, 3.8%
9.   BANGLADESH, 3.6%
10.   TAJIKISTAN, 3.5%
11.   CHINA, 3.2%
12.   NIGERIA, 3.2%
13.   UGANDA, 3.0%
14.   INDONESIA, 3.0%,
15.   MALI, 2.9%
16.   SYRIA, 2.7%
17.   DR OF CONGO, 2.7%
18.   REPUBLIC OF CONGO, 2.7%
19.   MOZAMBIQUE, 2.7%
20.   IRAN, 2.6%
21.   NEPAL, 2.5%
22.   THAILAND, 2.5%
23.   EGYPT, 2.5%
24.   NIGER, 2.4%
25.   ANGOLA, 2.4%
26.   TANZANIA, 2.4%
27.   CHAD, 2.4%
28.   LAOS, 2.4%
29.   BURKINA FASO, 2.3%
30.   SOUTH AFRICA, 2.3%
31.   RUSSIA, 2.2%
32.   PHILLIPINES, 2.1%
33.   BURMA/MYANMAR, 2.0%
34.   IVORY COAST, 2.0%
35.   TURKEY, 1.9%

36.	RWANDA, 1.9%
37.	LIBERIA, 1.9%
38.	SIERRA LEONE, 1.8%
39.	ALGERIA, 1.7%
40.	CAMBODIA, 1.7%
41.	CENTRAL AFRICAN REPUBLIC, 1.6%
42.	MALAWI, 1.6%
43.	IRAQ, 1.6%
44.	VIETNAM, 1.5%
45.	MAURITANIA, 1.2%
46.	CAMEROON, 1.2%
47.	KENYA, 1.1%
48.	LIBYA, 1.1%
49.	TOGO, 1.0%
50.	ZIMBABWE, 0.9%
51.	AZERBAIJAN, 0.9%
52.	COLOMBIA, 0.8%
53.	PAPUA NEW GUINEA, 0.8%
54.	JORDAN, 0.7%
55.	MADAGASCAR, 0.7%
56.	HAITI, 0.7%
57.	BURUNDI, 0.6%
58.	NICARAGUA, 0.6%
59.	LEBANON, 0.5%
60.	ARGENTINA, 0.5%
61.	PERU, 0.5%
62.	SRI LANKA, 0.5%
63.	ERITREA, 0.4%
64.	VENEZUELA, 0.4%
65.	EL SALVADOR, 0.4%
66.	KYRGYSTAN, 0.4%
67.	NORTH KOREA, 0.3%

68.   UZBEKISTAN, 0.3%
69.   UKRAINE, 0.3%
70.   BOSNIA/HERZEGOVINA, 0.3%
71.   MEXICO, 0.3%
72.   SOUTH KOREA, 0.3
73.   SOUTH SUDAN, 0.3%
74.   ROMANIA, 0.3%
75.   GUATEMALA, 0.3%
76.   PARAGUAY, 0.2%
77.   SERBIA, 0.2%
78.   UNITED KINGDOM, 0.1%
79.   TIMOR-LESTE, 0.1%
80.   PORTUGAL, 0.1%
81.   ALL OTHER COUNTRIES TIED FOR 81ST

Of all the factors, this is the one with the tightest causal connection with civilian gun ownership. Well-armed people have rarely been the subject of democide. Disarmed or unarmed people have often been the victims of mass murder. Don B. Kates wrote an important article about this subject.[122] He argues that, contrary to what some "experts" believe, arming citizens has and will have a deterrent effect on genocide. Kates cites examples of genocides that were preceded by gun confiscation and argues that, with the possible exception of the Holocaust, arming groups targeted for extermination would work and in the case of the Croatians, did work. I might add that no group targeted for extinction has ever declined arms when proffered.

---

[122] "Genocide, Self Defense and the Right to Bear Arms," 29 *Hamline L. Rev.* 501 (Summer, 2006).

Legal scholar Stephen P. Halbrook, after detailing the many efforts to disarm Jews in Germany before the Holocaust writes: "If the Nazi experience teaches anything, it teaches that totalitarian governments will attempt to disarm their subjects to extinguish any ability to fight crimes against humanity." [123] During the Rwandan genocide, there was active resistance, however, the targets were often short of weapons and on several occasions when they had guns, resisted until they ran out of bullets.[124] This is precisely why citizens need so-called "assault rifles" (semiautomatics) and high-capacity magazines and plenty of ammunition. It's not about hunting deer as Andrew Cuomo famously quipped; it's about resisting mass murder!

Even the hard case of the Holocaust argues for the efficacy of arming the targets of democide and genocide. The heroic Warsaw Uprising of 1943, shows that even a poorly armed guerrilla group facing a well-equipped modern army, can inflict severe damage on the enemy. About 1,000 poorly armed guerrilla fighters held off 10,000 German troops for 28 days.[125] Had they been fully armed with "assault rifles," they would have likely survived much longer and inflicted more casualties on the enemy and perhaps even inspired more resistance among the population generally. Even if the Jews targeted for horrific extermination only had a ghost of a chance, they nevertheless had a natural right to attempt armed resistance.

---

[123] *Death by Gun Control,* p. 103.
[124] *Id.* at 123 et seq.
[125] *Id.* at 54.

The two groups most victimized by American government historically, slaves and American Indians, were systematically disarmed. Slaves were generally barred from firearms ownership while American Indians were frequently disarmed by American troops, most famously at the Wounded Knee Massacre.[126] So yes, it *can* happen here because it *has* happened here!

Thus, I propose a new comprehensive system to rank each country in the world by its overall degree of violence with government violence by a conservative estimate counting 50%, homicides counting 20%[127], combat casualties counting 15%, democide counting 10%,[128] and terrorism counting 5%. A complete ranking of countries appears in Chapter 4.

To sum up:

Government violence (50%): United States ranks 17th best in the world.

Domestic Homicide (20%): United States ranks 76th best.

---

[126] See *McDonald v. City of Chicago*, 561 U.S. 742 (2010) on efforts to deprive freed slaves of the right to bear arms after the Civil War; https://en.wikipedia.org/wiki/Wounded_Knee_Massac re

[127] See R. Keinfeld, supra (noting that homicide takes more lives than war in the typical year).

[128] *Id.* (Urging that "one-sided violence" (democide) be counted in statistics that compare violence among countries).

War casualties (15%): United States ranks tied for 1st in the world.

Democide (10%): United States ranks tied for 1st in the world.

Terrorism (5%): United States ranks 135th best in the world.

Weighing each factor according to this formula, we reach the conclusion that the United States, with by far the most civilian gun ownership in the world, is not even close to being the most violent nation on Earth. In fact, the United States, is, according to this revolutionary new standard, the 27th most peaceful country on Earth out of 165.

27th at first glance might not sound very impressive, but keep in mind that most of the countries ahead of the United States are not at all comparable and most are tiny European monocultural countries or isolated islands. Also keep in mind that the crime problem in the United States, the major negative factor in the United States ranking, is concentrated in certain cities and neighborhoods devastated by progressive big government and Great Society policies and that the vast majority of urban, suburban and rural America has crime levels that approximate levels in the tiny monocultural European countries the gun controllers love to brag about. The other factor that lowers the overall rating of the United States, terrorism, is almost entirely the fault of government policy: endless and mindless foreign intervention.

ADT has a very useful crime mapping tool[129] that allows us to visualize the point made here that crime in America is extremely *localized*[130] and tends to be more common where there are *fewer* guns per capita. Using their tool, you can quickly spot every county in any given state whose rate of violent crime is twice the national average. For example, in the large, diverse, heavily populated states of New York and Pennsylvania, only one county in Pennsylvania (Philadelphia) and five contiguous counties in New York (New York City), have unusually high crime rates. The violent crime rate in Bronx County, one of the five counties in New York City, is eight times higher than the violent crime rate in rural, Upstate Wyoming County near Buffalo.[131] Even in Bronx County, the most violent county in New York City, the crime rate varies widely. The South Bronx (zip code 10454) has a violent crime rate *13 times higher* than the North Bronx (zip code 10470), even though both neighborhoods have the *exact same federal, state and local gun laws* and it is highly likely that the lower crime zip code has a higher rate of gun ownership.[132]

Obviously, the high crime rate in the South Bronx is related to the progressive's failed war on drugs, however,

---

[129] https://www.adt.com/crime

[130] See, R. McMaken, "Five Tricks Gun-Control Advocates Play," *Mises.org* (Nov. 1, 2016).

[131]

https://www.criminaljustice.ny.gov/crimnet/ojsa/coun tycrimestats.htm (2021 data).

[132] Source for crime rates: CrimeGrade.org.

the gun control movement is deliberately obtuse about the causes of violence as that would distract from their continual scapegoating of guns. Although gun controllers talk endlessly about *the fact* of gun crimes in America, their almost complete lack of curiosity about *the actual causes* of crime in America and their utter lack of interest in *doing anything* about those root causes is a Freudian slip. Because they view guns as a panopathogen[133] and gun control as a panacea, they are genetically incapable of addressing the causes of violence. To do so would imply that gun control is *not* the panacea they have been saying it is for fifty years.

Probably the single most fixable cause of gun violence in the United States and abroad is the war on drugs.[134] This war was started by progressive Democrat Woodrow Wilson in 1914 and, aside from legalizing marijuana so they can make money from Americans getting high and hungry, there are no proposals among leading progressives and Democrats to end that war. Progressives would rather use guns to scapegoat all those "mass shootings" caused by the drug war so they can advance their gun control agenda.

New Hampshire, a state with constitutional carry, has zero high-crime counties. Nearby Maine also has zero high crime counties. On the opposite end of the country, Montana, which leads the United States in guns per

---

[133] A wonderful term used by my late friend Thomas Szasz in his masterpiece, *Ceremonial Chemistry: The Ritual Persecution of Drugs, Addicts, and Pushers* (1974).
[134] Ostrowski, James (1990) "The Moral and Practical Case for Drug Legalization," *Hofstra Law Review*: Vol. 18: Issue. 3, Article 5.

capita,[135] has zero high-crime counties. Wyoming, second in gun ownership, and Idaho, fourth in gun ownership, likewise have zero high-crime counties. Turning to the Southeast, Tennessee, a constitutional carry state and 14th in gun ownership, has only five high-crime counties out of 95, four of which are in urban areas where gun ownership tends to be lower than in rural counties. Since gun policies are both *national* and *statewide*, yet high crime areas are extremely *localized* and not only do not correlate with regulatory policies but tend to be located where gun ownership is the lowest, this evidence shows that *gun ownership per se does not cause crime* but many other factors, all ignored by the gun control movement, do cause violent crime.

But most importantly, remember our purpose here has been to refute the main lie of the gun controllers, that because of the Second Amendment and the resulting widespread civilian gun ownership in America, the United States is an unusually or especially violent country. I have proven conclusively that this is false and that, in fact, the United States is not remotely the most dangerous country on Earth and in fact is in the upper twenty percent of the most peaceful countries on Earth even though it is a large, diverse country with an open southern border that violent drug gangs can cross with impunity.

My ranking of the United States as one of the more peaceful countries on Earth and *the most peaceful large and diverse country*, is buttressed by many other data points. If we closely observe *what people do* with what they value the most, themselves and their families, the overwhelming

---

[135] Source: Ammo.com.

empirical evidence is that *the masses* agree with the conclusion of this chapter: the United States is, apart from certain dangerous neighborhoods, a relatively peaceful country. For instance, the United States is filled with people wealthy enough to live in many other countries but relatively few people choose to so move. The opposite is true. There is a massive movement of people *into the United States*, including legal immigrants, illegal immigrants, refugees and asylum seekers. The United States is third in the world in tourism with fifty million higher-income travelers each year.[136] The United States is a leader in foreign investment which suggests that shrewd investors do not view the United States as violent and unstable. The United States also has the largest economy on Earth. Refugees from violent and unstable countries without a well-armed civilian population often choose to relocate to the United States. See Table No. 7

---

[136] *Source:* Wikipedia.

Table No. 7

Refugees Vote With Their Feet for the Second Amendment

Countries of origin for refugees to the U. S. (2010-2020) *Source:* Migration policy.org	Number of refugees	Rank in civilian gun ownership (USA—1) *Source:* Wikipedia	Guns per 100 people (USA—120.5) *Source:* Wikipedia
Myanmar	125,137	179	1.6
Iraq	109,412	29	19.6
Bhutan	77,409	196	0.8
DR. Congo	70,409	186	1.2
Somalia	54,211	66	12.4
Iran	22,573	106	7.3
Syria	22,163	99	8.2
Cuba	20,020	172	2.1
Ukraine	19,237	88	9.9
Eritrea	18,223	213	0.4
	Average	133.4	6.35

Thus, observing what people actually *do*, as opposed to what they *say*, we can conclude that people's observed behavior in a world of choice and their demonstrated preferences,[137] the most reliable means of determining what people actually prefer, show conclusively that the United States is not only not the unusually violent country gun controllers pretend it to be, but it is in fact the relatively peaceful, geographically and demographically large, diverse and wide open country that this new and pathbreaking ranking system shows that it is.

As previously discussed, there are isolated pockets of violent street crime, unrelated to the degree of civilian gun ownership in those neighborhoods. Indeed, those high-crime neighborhoods have far fewer guns than low-crime neighborhoods have. Lest the author be accused of biased reporting in this regard, let me quote from sources that, not only have no axe to grind in this regard, but are themselves organizations friendly to strict gun

---

[137] "The concept of demonstrated preference is simply this: that actual choice reveals, or demonstrates, a man's preferences; that is, that his preferences are deducible from what he has chosen in action. Thus, if a man chooses to spend an hour at a concert rather than a movie, we deduce that the former was preferred, or ranked higher on his value scale. Similarly, if a man spends five dollars on a shirt we deduce that he preferred purchasing the shirt to any other uses he could have found for the money. This concept of preference, rooted in real choices, forms the keystone of the logical structure of economic analysis, and particularly of utility and welfare analysis." Murray N. Rothbard: *Toward a Reconstruction of Utility and Welfare Economics* (1956).

control laws. Here is the government of Canada's Travel Advisory for the United States:

Violent crime

"Within large urban areas, violent crime more commonly *occurs in poor neighbourhoods*, particularly from dusk to dawn. It often involves intoxication. Incidents of violent crime are mainly carried out by gangs or members of organized crime groups but may also be perpetrated by lone individuals. Although *violent crime rarely affects tourists*: be mindful of your surroundings at all time(s); verify official neighbourhood crime statistics before planning an outing; if threatened by robbers, stay calm and don't resist" (Emphasis added.)[138]

Here is the United Kingdom's Travel Advisory for the United States:

Violent crime

"*Tourists are rarely involved in violent and gun crime, but take care in unfamiliar areas.* Avoid walking through quieter areas alone, especially at night. You can find public advisories and information about recent incidents on the websites of local law

---

[138] https://travel.gc.ca/destinations/united-states

enforcement authorities. *Incidents of mass shooting can happen but are a very small percentage of homicide deaths.* Read the US Department of Homeland Security advice on what to do in an active shooter incident.

"Research your destination before travelling and follow the advice of local authorities. *Crime associated with illegal drugs* is a major issue in Mexican states bordering Arizona, California, New Mexico and Texas. Some foreign nationals have been victims of crime in the border regions, but there is no evidence to suggest they have been targeted because of their nationality." (Emphasis added)

These neutral reports from pro-gun control governments provide additional proof of what is actually common knowledge: with respect to street crime, the United States is a relatively safe country with isolated pockets of violent crime primarily fueled by the progressive Democratic war on drug users started by Woodrow Wilson.

Allow me to present my final piece of evidence in support of the thesis of this chapter: *the behavior of those who most fervently support gun control.* It is no surprise that in a country whose governing political ideology for over a hundred years is progressivism and whose schools and media are dominated by progressives, gun control is widely popular among low information voters.[139] There

---

[139] en.wikipedia.org/wiki/Low_information_voter

is a much smaller but still sizable group of Americans who are particularly active in the gun control movement in some manner. They may be volunteer activists, paid staffers for any of the 47 gun control organizations in the country, donors to such organizations, or even elected officials or other government employees who actively support gun control. There is no official estimate of the number of hard core supporters of gun control. Let's make a conservative estimate of 100,000 people.

These are people who in many cases are wealthy enough to be able to relocate if they did not prefer their current country of residency. There are well over a hundred countries with stricter gun control laws than the United States and much lower rates of civilian gun ownership. One of these countries, Canada, is within driving distance of 49 states and has notoriously liberal immigration policies and a first-world economy. English is one of the two official languages there. Another strict gun control country, Mexico, is also within driving distance of 49 states and is known to allow Americans to relocate there and 1.6 million have done so.[140]

We come to the crux of the matter. How many American gun control advocates have *voted with their feet* to escape what they view as senseless and mindless and nightmarish and ubiquitous violence? While many Hollywood actresses threatened to leave the country if so and so was elected President and never did, there is no evidence of *any* gun control activists threatening to do so or actually doing so. Thus, not only have I proven through a comprehensive *statistical analysis,* and by a comprehensive *demonstrated preference analysis,* that the

---

[140] *Source:* internationalcitizens.com.

United States is not an unusually violent country, but, finally, I have proven that the very people who make this charge, *choose to remain in the hellhole country they disparage when they could easily relocate.* Indeed, a large number of gun control activists actually chose to move *to the United States* from a country with strict gun control and a low level of civilian gun ownership, where they are now free, thanks in large part to the right to free speech protected by the right to bear arms, and no shortage of ingratitude and chutzpah, to call for the repeal of the Second Amendment.

To sum up, in Chapter 2, I proved that the leading cause of gun violence in the United States is the government itself and that this is true by an astronomical multiplier. In this Chapter I have proven that, compared to other countries, the United States is a relatively safe, large and diverse country, in spite of its wide-open southern border and self-inflicted drug war, and a large underclass manufactured by numerous failed progressive big government programs, except for certain neighborhoods where failed government policies have produced massive crime waves, especially since the birth of the Great Society in 1965.

Thus, I have, with two brand-new comprehensive statistics, refuted and destroyed the main premises of the gun control movement in America. Good riddance!

4.　　Ranking Countries by Their
Overall Level of Violence

Using the formula set forth above, we can now for the first time rank the 165 largest countries on the planet by their degree of overall violence. See Table No. 9. The total score and ranking was determined by converting the five factors outlined in Chapter 3 into numbers, then weighting the numbers according to their relative importance as explained in Chapter 3.

The United States places 27th out of 165 in overall peace. This puts the lie to the main thesis of gun control which paints the United States as an extremely violent country because of its right to bear arms. On the contrary, the country with by far the highest civilian gun ownership is the most peaceful large country on the planet. Most of the countries ranked higher than the United States are not comparable for one reason or another. They are small, mono-cultural European nations, isolated islands or protectorates of the United States.

Don't get me wrong. The United States is not a utopia. It is a deeply flawed country that has strayed from the libertarian roots that made it great. Its dominant ideology now is a toxic stew of progressive big government, circa 1913 and radical egalitarian leftism, circa 2014. The solution is not more government gun violence but far less. See, Chapter Five for concrete proposals to increase liberty in America.

Now, turning to the rest of this violent world, this new list of countries by their degree of violence opens the door to finally understanding the underlying major causes of violence in this world, to set the stage for a pathbreaking new global violence control movement.

The correlation between violence and the absence of a right to bear arms is not perfect since factors beyond that right can exert a major impact on violence. These include: ideology, historical conflicts, poorly drawn national borders, intervention by foreign powers and other factors. Nevertheless, the Global Violence Index is loaded with countries notable for their violence, instability or repressive, authoritarian regimes, and the absence of a well-armed civilian population. Examples are legion and include:

Table No. 8

COUNTRY	OVERALL VIOLENCE RANKING/165	GUNS PER 100 PEOPLE
Syria	164	8.2
Sudan	163	6.6
Venezuela	162	18.5
Myanmar	161	1.6
Somalia	160	12.4
Nigeria	159	3.2
Iran	157	7.3
Ethiopia	156	0.4
DR Congo	152	1.2
India	144	5.3
Bangladesh	140	0.4
China	130	3.6
South Africa	129	9.7

All these countries lack both a legal right to bear arms and a well-armed civilian population. In their absence, violence, crime, instability and repression have thrived. In sharp contrast, the best-armed nation on Earth, the United States, in spite of many countervailing factors such as its abandonment of its founding libertarian philosophy around 1913, is a large, diverse, stable, peaceful, and economically successful country whose relative success in an imperfect world is verified by the millions of people from all over the world who risk their lives to get here.

All this data-crunching and ranking is merely a prologue to the important task of making this a more peaceful and less violent world in which to live for eight billion people. Chapter Five will explain how we can do that.

Countries Ranked by Overall Violence

Table No. 9

Global Violence Index Rank	Country	Government Violence Score From Human Freedom Index	Homicide Rate (100k)	War Casualties Rank	Democide Risk--Early Warning Project	Terrorism Risk From Global Terrorism Index	Global Violence Index Score
1	Switzerland	9.01	0.59	80	0	2205	100
2	Denmark	8.83	1.01	80	0	158	98.81
3	Ireland	8.79	0.87	80	0	291	98.33
4	Luxembourg	8.71	0.34	80	0	0	97.85
5	Iceland	8.73	0.89	80	0	0	97.77
6	New Zealand	8.88	0.74	80	0	3776	97.4
7	Estonia	8.75	2.12	80	0	0	97.28
8	Finland	8.7	1.63	80	0	0	96.97
9	Sweden	8.75	1.08	80	0	2307	96.51
10	Taiwan	8.56	0.82	78	0	0	95.38
11	Netherlands	8.57	0.59	80	0	2120	94.75
12	Australia	8.52	0.89	80	0	1830	94.14
13	Norway	8.58	0.47	80	0	3514	94.1
14	Czechia	8.38	0.45	80	0	0	93.81
15	Canada	8.55	1.76	80	0	3275	93.12
16	Malta	8.37	1.59	80	0	0	93.01
17	Japan	8.4	0.26	80	0	2398	92.72
18	Belgium	8.33	1.69	80	0	0	92.47
19	Latvia	8.45	4.36	80	0	0	92.34
20	Portugal	8.27	0.79	80	0.001	0	92.05
21	Lithuania	8.39	4.57	80	0	508	91.19
22	United Kingdom	8.39	1.2	80	0.001	3840	90.96
23	Germany	8.37	0.95	80	0	4242	90.85
24	South Korea	8.12	0.59	80	0	0	90.59
25	Austria	8.24	0.97	80	0	2677	90.21
26	Cyprus	8.15	1.26	73	0	1392	88.41
27	United States	8.39	4.96	80	0	4799	88.39
28	Slovenia	7.9	0.48	80	0	0	88
29	Spain	8.03	0.62	80	0	2712	87.86
30	Slovakia	8.04	1.14	80	0	2784	87.63
31	Italy	7.95	0.57	80	0	3290	86.58
32	Singapore	7.75	0.16	80	0	0	86.38
33	Croatia	7.96	0.58	66	0	0	86.05
34	Cabo Verde	8	6.18	80	0	0	85.84
35	Montenegro	7.8	2.23	80	0	0	85.76
36	Hong Kong	7.7	0.65	80	0	0	85.49
37	Poland	7.69	0.73	80	0	0	85.32
38	Seychelles	7.85	4.7	80	0	0	84.91
39	Bulgaria	7.68	1.3	80	0	0	84.87

Countries Ranked by Overall Violence

Global Violence Index Rank	Country	Government Violence Score From Human Freedom Index	Homicide Rate (100k)	War Casualties Rank	Democide Risk--Early Warning Project	Terrorism Risk From Global Terrorism Index	Global Violence Index Score
40	France	7.86	1.2	80	0	4419	84.45
41	North Macedonia	7.64	1.2	80	0	0	84.44
42	Romania	7.9	1.28	68	0.003	682	84.19
43	Chile	8.16	4.4	76	0	6619	84.11
44	Costa Rica	8.04	11.26	80	0	0	83.32
45	Gibraltar	7.61	2.92	80	0	0	83.06
46	Moldova	7.66	4.1	80	0	0	82.97
47	Uruguay	7.96	12.06	80	0	826	81.39
48	Albania	7.67	2.29	65	0	0	81.35
49	Georgia	7.8	2.22	53	0	0	80.72
50	Armenia	7.99	1.69	39	0	0	80.7
51	Barbados	7.72	9.77	80	0	0	80.34
52	Greece	7.49	0.94	80	0	4793	79.92
53	Mongolia	7.43	6.18	80	0	0	78.97
54	Ghana	7.19	2.09	80	0	0	78.49
55	Fiji	7.16	2.31	80	0	0	78
56	Hungary	7.24	2.49	75	0	0	77.92
56	Timor-Leste	7.26	4.1	80	0.001	0	77.92
58	Dominican Republic	7.56	10.05	74	0	0	77.13
59	Panama	7.57	9.39	67	0	0	76.33
60	Bosnia and Herzegovina	7.33	1.17	56	0.003	0	75.54
61	Suriname	7.07	5.43	80	0	0	75.07
62	Serbia	7.14	1.23	62	0.002	0	74.57
63	Ecuador	7.03	5.8	80	0	2198	73.05
64	Bhutan	6.69	1.19	80	0	0	72.99
65	Peru	7.56	7.91	63	0.005	3856	72.87
66	Paraguay	7.06	7.14	80	0.002	1605	72.52
67	Benin	6.86	1.13	80	0	4840	72.18
68	Botswana	7.31	15.25	80	0	0	72.16
69	Bolivia	6.83	6.22	79	0	0	71.52
70	Kyrgyzstan	6.64	2.19	80	0.004	0	70.88
71	Guinea-Bissau	6.51	1.15	80	0	0	70.85
72	Namibia	7.31	17.68	80	0	0	70.73
73	Malawi	6.83	1.81	80	0.016	0	70.64
74	Malaysia	6.66	2.13	72	0	1357	69.77
75	Argentina	6.85	5.32	80	0.005	2875	69.61
76	Bahamas	7.82	31.96	80	0	0	68.44
77	Israel	7.43	1.49	24	0	5489	67.98
78	Gambia	6.64	9.1	80	0	0	67.72

Countries Ranked by Overall Violence

Global Violence Index Rank	Country	Government Violence Score From Human Freedom Index	Homicide Rate (100k)	War Casualties Rank	Democide Risk--Early Warning Project	Terrorism Risk From Global Terrorism Index	Global Violence Index Score
79	Senegal	6.71	0.27	51	0	1108	67.69
80	Kuwait	6.25	1.82	80	0	0	67.32
81	Kazakhstan	6.4	5.06	80	0	0	67.21
82	Gabon	6.5	8	80	0	0	66.68
83	Guyana	6.74	14.25	80	0	0	65.88
84	Jordan	6.32	1.36	80	0.007	2033	65.61
85	Trinidad and Tobago	7.45	30.65	80	0	0	64.75
86	Zambia	6.21	5.37	80	0	0	64.74
87	Madagascar	6.36	7.7	80	0.007	0	63.56
88	Cote d'Ivoire	6.48	9.5	80	0	3747	63.31
89	Sierra Leone	6.51	1.73	59	0.018	0	62.44
90	United Arab Emirates	5.73	0.46	80	0	1241	61.11
91	Brunei	5.65	0.49	80	0	0	60.87
92	Papua New Guinea	6.88	9.75	37	0.008	0	60.35
93	Guatemala	7.09	22.5	57	0.003	0	60.23
94	Brazil	6.92	27.38	80	0	599	59.93
95	Oman	5.56	0.27	80	0	0	59.91
96	Jamaica	7.56	43.85	80	0	0	58.28
97	Bahrain	5.47	0.52	80	0	826	58.19
98	Nepal	6.71	2.3	47	0.025	4134	58.18
99	Liberia	6.39	3.26	49	0.019	0	57.99
100	Morocco	5.48	1.42	80	0	757	57.82
101	Qatar	5.39	0.37	80	0	0	57.8
102	Belarus	5.48	2.39	80	0	0	57.7
103	Togo	6.2	9	80	0.01	4915	57.23
104	Tunisia	6.22	3.06	41	0	3989	56.54
104	Mauritania	5.34	1.2	80	0	291	56.54
106	Cambodia	6.08	1.84	54	0.017	0	56.48
107	Haiti	6.37	6.68	38	0.007	0	56.43
108	Indonesia	6.62	0.43	48	0.03	5502	56.42
109	Tanzania	6.16	6.48	80	0.024	4065	55.53
110	Ukraine	6.72	6.18	6	0.003	1535	54.96
111	Sri Lanka	6.13	2.42	43	0.005	4839	54.55
112	Thailand	6.67	2.58	33	0.025	5430	54.14
113	Rwanda	5.89	2.58	61	0.019	826	54.11
114	Kenya	6.57	4.93	31	0.011	6163	53.95
115	Belize	6.82	37.79	80	0	0	52.94
116	Vietnam	5.51	1.53	69	0.015	227	52.92
117	Djibouti	5.32	6.5	80	0	3800	51.06

Countries Ranked by Overall Violence

Global Violence Index Rank	Country	Government Violence Score From Human Freedom Index	Homicide Rate (100k)	War Casualties Rank	Democide Risk--Early Warning Project	Terrorism Risk From Global Terrorism Index	Global Violence Index Score
118	Burkina Faso	6.57	1.25	22	0.023	8564	50.25
119	Nicaragua	5.48	7.19	58	0.006	0	49.37
120	Mozambique	6.51	3.51	26	0.027	7330	48.76
121	Lebanon	5.74	2.49	29	0.005	3400	48.05
122	Niger	6.29	4.43	34	0.024	7616	47.58
123	Laos	5.34	4.5	71	0.024	0	47.56
124	Angola	5.76	4.85	44	0.024	158	47.27
125	Azerbaijan	5.65	2.2	21	0.009	0	46.75
126	Philippines	6.46	6.46	17	0.021	6328	46.71
127	Eswatini	5.07	11.56	80	0	1058	46.7
128	Congo	5.41	9.3	80	0.027	0	46.56
129	South Africa	6.92	36.4	64	0.023	826	46.19
130	China	5.15	0.53	70	0.032	0	45.59
131	Lesotho	6.49	43.56	80	0	0	45.55
132	Saudi Arabia	4.53	1.27	80	0	2387	45.47
133	Zimbabwe	4.86	7.48	80	0.009	0	45.14
134	Honduras	6.72	38.93	42	0	0	43.95
135	Tajikistan	5.44	1.64	60	0.035	3438	43.81
136	Uganda	5.75	10.52	46	0.03	3599	40.74
137	Cameroon	5.3	1.39	30	0.012	7347	39.61
138	Turkey	5.63	2.59	14	0.019	5600	39.32
139	El Salvador	6.85	52.02	55	0.004	0	39.29
140	Bangladesh	5.51	2.37	36	0.036	3827	39.27
141	Mexico	6.55	29.07	5	0.003	1578	39.17
142	Russia	5.81	8.21	16	0.022	3799	38.93
143	Colombia	6.54	25.34	15	0.008	6697	38.91
144	India	6.29	3.08	12	0.053	7175	37.86
145	Algeria	4.82	1.36	45	0.017	4083	37.45
146	Mali	5.9	10.2	23	0.029	8412	35.78
147	Guinea	5.21	8.7	52	0.045	0	35.13
148	Libya	4.94	2.5	20	0.011	4730	34.54
149	Burundi	4.85	6.05	19	0.006	4051	32.72
150	Central African Republic	5.34	20.12	27	0.016	3194	30.03
151	Chad	4.99	9.1	25	0.024	6168	28.33
152	DR Congo	5.48	13.6	10	0.027	6872	27.66
153	Egypt	4.24	2.55	50	0.025	6632	27.32
154	Pakistan	5.49	3.88	13	0.061	8160	25.5
155	Comoros	5.45	60	80	0	0	23.29
156	Ethiopia	5.2	8.79	3	0.051	3044	22.59

Countries Ranked by Overall Violence

Global Violence Index Rank	Country	Government Violence Score From Human Freedom Index	Homicide Rate (100k)	War Casualties Rank	Democide Risk--Early Warning Project	Terrorism Risk From Global Terrorism Index	Global Violence Index Score
157	Iran	4.03	2.5	35	0.026	5688	22.35
158	Iraq	4.73	10.07	4	0.016	8139	21.35
159	Nigeria	5.96	34.52	11	0.032	8065	19.41
160	Somalia	4.49	4.3	9	0.038	8463	17.55
161	Myanmar	3.88	2.9	18	0.02	7977	17.13
162	Venezuela	4.22	36.69	40	0.004	3409	11.8
163	Sudan	3.81	5.15	7	0.057	0	9.17
164	Syria	2.96	0.88	1	0.027	8161	2.34
165	Yemen	3.43	6.77	8	0.059	5616	0

5.   Replacing Gun Control with Violence Control

For way too many years, those who support the right to bear arms have been playing defense against the well-funded and much better organized gun control movement. Since progressivism replaced libertarianism as the ruling ideology of American government around 1913, and gun control is a quintessentially progressive program (use of aggressive government force to improve society), the gun control movement has been swimming with the tide. Since the media's predominant ideology is knee-jerk progressive, the media has exhibited a clear bias in favor of gun control for decades. Finally, since progressivism is also the default ideology of K-12 government schools and their mostly Democratic teachers, millions of young people graduate each year favorably disposed to gun control.

At the same time and for the same reasons, the notion that the primary purpose of the right to bear arms is to deter government tyranny has been suppressed or ignored by the media and the schools and the politicians as has the fact the Second Amendment *works* in that regard.

The publication of *The Second Amendment Works: A Primer on How to Protect our Most Important Right* in 2022, marked the moment the Second Amendment movement started to turn the tables on the gun control movement by reframing the issue and marshalling massive evidence that the Second Amendment works!

Now, with the publication of this sequel to *The Second Amendment Works*, we have new research and statistics that definitively expose and refute the main lies and distortions of the gun control movement and prove that the main threat of violence against innocent people in any society is the government itself and that the right to bear arms has worked in America to deter and restrain that threat. The statistical evidence for these propositions is clear and undeniable.

The *intellectual* work has been completed. What remains, however, is the critical task of *education*, which in this case primarily involves debamboozling tens of millions of Americans who have been lied to for generations about gun control and the right to bear arms. I briefly outline a workable plan below.

THE PLAN

1. Widespread distribution of these books to gun owners in America
2. Distribution of the books to every member of Congress, every state legislator, governor and every federal and state judge in America
3. Distribution to journalists and professors
4. Podcasts that summarize the two books for wide distribution on all social media platforms
5. Fliers that summarize the case—two page, one page, postcard, refrigerator

magnet, business card. Distribution door to door to every home in America
6. House signs and bumper stickers
7. TV and radio ads
8. Victory—defined as constitutional carry of handguns, rifles and shotguns in every state
9. A global right to bear arms
10. Instead of the gun confiscation movement, create a true movement against violence and make the world a more peaceful place: **a violence control movement!**

PROPOSED GLOBAL RIGHT TO BEAR ARMS.

"Every adult human being on the planet Earth has a natural human right to fabricate, buy or otherwise acquire the means of self-defense against criminals, terrorists, oppressive governments or any form of organized crime, which means shall include but not be limited to rifles, shotguns and handguns and the ammunition for such weapons; and no government may interfere with this natural right, directly or indirectly and no government may require that any person seek prior permission or a license or permit from the government to fabricate, purchase or otherwise acquire said means of self-defense, unless such person is actually and currently being punished under law for a serious crime of violence such as terrorism, murder, rape, child abuse, robbery or kidnapping."

HOW TO REDUCE VIOLENCE IN THE WORLD

The gun control movement seeks to do the impossible: reduce gun violence by vastly increasing the amount of government gun violence. Their math does not work. It's a movement that seeks to reduce violence in the world by massively increasing violence. Now that we have a proper understanding of the true nature, extent and types of violence in the world, we are finally well-positioned to propose policy changes that would reduce violence in the world. The gun control movement, by disguising its own true nature as a movement that seeks to *increase* violence in the world, both directly and indirectly, and, as a movement that seeks to scapegoat lawful gun owners as the cause of violence in society, and that therefore systematically ignores, covers up or obfuscates the true nature and variety and causes and perpetrators of crime, including governments (the leading perpetrators of violence on the planet), has been a tremendous hindrance to those who sincerely wish to reduce violence in the world and move the world towards peace and liberty.

Now that the gun control movement has been exposed for what it is, a movement that proposes to massively increase violence against citizens who wish to own guns by violently disarming them by the hundreds of millions, and therefore leaving them defenseless against criminals, governments, terrorists, private armies and criminal organizations of every type, and therefore allow and encourage such entities to increase their violent activities with impunity, and now that the various forms of violence in the world have been delineated and explored, those truly interested in peace and liberty are now free to propose solutions that will substantially reduce violence in the world in all its major forms. This new movement for peace and liberty can now do what the gun control movement has pretended to do for decades: issue specific proposals to make the world a more peaceful place to live.

It has already been shown in this book that *government* is implicated in all five major types of violence in the world: crime, government violence, war, terrorism and democide.

Crime. Though crime, by definition, is non-governmental, numerous failed government policies are implicated in the relatively large degree of violent crime in the United States. These policies include the war on drugs, failed welfare programs, failed government schools, and failed economic policies that make it extremely difficult for poorly educated, poorly raised, and largely unskilled young people to enter the workforce and progress upwards. To reduce crime, we can enact constitutional carry, end the drug war and begin to roll back the various failed progressive programs that engender crime.

Government violence. By definition, this is the government itself committing violence by exceeding its legitimate functions of defending the country from foreign invasion, keeping the peace and providing just dispute resolution. That being the case, the solution is obvious. Shrink the colossal and ever-growing progressive state of America and move towards the original model of the minimal state. Phase out the welfare/warfare/transfer state, end the global military empire and bring the troops home.[141] Exit the Fed[142] and have pay-as-you-go budgets that don't borrow from future Americans to pay for unsustainable programs today. End the failed experiment in tax-supported compulsory schooling (daytime juvenile detention and indoctrination centers) and end all subsidies to "education" across the board. Allow the free market to operate in health care in the aftermath of the obvious and catastrophic failure of government during the Covid Lockdown.

End welfare programs that break up families or discourage family-formation. When children are the product, not of marriage, but financial calculation, their prospects are not bright. Their chances of drifting into a life of crime are quite good.

Phase out all transfer payments. In the United States, government seizes as much as forty percent of our

---

[141] Downsizing government should, of course, be done in a humanitarian manner with a priority on immediately increasing economic liberty so as to provide job and business opportunities for the masses and slashing all taxes, especially payroll taxes, on the poor and working classes so as to *immediately* put more money into their paychecks and pockets. The poor and working class need a "living" cost of government.

[142] Ron Paul, *End the Fed* (2009).

income.[143] About half of those funds are then transferred to other people,[144] directly or indirectly, often including the same people from whom it was seized, minus of course the massive transaction costs of such transfers. As I explained in *Progressivism: A Primer*, there are three parties to the transaction, the taxpayer, tax collector and tax consumer. Each party has a lower incentive to work productively. Thus, phasing out the welfare state and transfer state will not only immediately create a less violent and more peaceful society, but would also lead to much greater economic productivity by increasing the incentive of all in society to work *productively*, instead of working *aggressively* or benefiting from those who do. This would help the poor by increasing overall wealth, increasing job and business opportunities and wages and *drastically lowering the cost of living*.

If we did half of these things, the United States would quickly climb to number one in the Cato-Frazier rankings, most importantly reflecting a real increase in peace and liberty and a massive decrease in violence against citizens by the government.

War. Allow borders to be adjusted to match the reality on the ground. A huge number of civil wars and insurgencies result from the existence of national borders that make no sense and force groups and nations that are hostile to each other to fight over control of the government. The solution is to allow free and fair elections of secession so that borders can be redrawn to

---

[143] https://www.statista.com/statistics/268356/ratio-of-government-expenditure-to-gross-domestic-product-gdp-in-the-united-states/
[144] USGovernmentSpending.com.

reflect the facts on the ground. These ethnic, racial and religious civil wars have gone on for too long with the obvious solution ignored by the obtuse "experts" on war and conflict. The solution is simple: allow discrete groups to secede from larger polities dominated by hostile groups and nations.[145]

The model is Norway's secession from Sweden in 1905. Norwegians voted 368,208 to 184 to leave and no further fuss about the matter has been heard in the intervening 119 years![146] Most of Ireland seceded from the United Kingdom in 1921 and peace has prevailed in that part of Ireland ever since. It's utterly amazing what happens when borders match the reality on the ground and not some fantasy in the minds of politicians, academics and court historians.

War is a policy of the government itself so, although government cannot always predict, prevent or deter attacks and invasions from other countries, governments can adopt policies and practices that sharply decrease the risk of war:

1. Non-intervention into the internal affairs of other countries
2. Free trade (*not* corporatist managed trade)—"If goods don't cross borders, troops will." (Frederic Bastiat.)

---

[145] See, *Secession, State and Liberty,* Ed. by Gordon, David (2002).

[146] *Source:* Wikipedia.

3. Stop treating borders that no longer make any sense as sacrosanct. Allow groups and nations to vote by plebiscite to peacefully secede. There is *nothing* sacred about borders and boundaries. Many of them are arbitrary and based on where some army stopped conquering territory during some ancient or modern war. Borders must cohere with the current ethnic, religious and racial realities on the ground. This is blatantly obvious, but the post-Enlightenment mind continues to deny this obvious truth. Emerson carries the day here: "A foolish consistency is the hobgoblin of little minds."

4. Adopt a Global Right to Bear Arms to create political stability, encourage economic freedom and deter tyranny, democide and genocide.

Terrorism. Terrorism is the weapon of the weak, usually responding to some real or perceived oppression by a government. There are a number of steps that can be taken to reduce the risk of terrorism. These include ending foreign intervention, establishing a global right to bear arms, and allowing persecuted minority groups to break off and form their own countries peacefully through plebiscite.[147]

Democide. Democide is usually a government program or a program of a would-be government. Some of the ideas already discussed would be useful in deterring democide including the right to secede and a global right to bear arms. The classical liberals propounded the natural human right of freedom of movement. We do need to recognize and protect the right of people to flee tyrannies and find new homes, consistent with private property rights and the right of nations to control their own internal affairs, elections and budgets. As I have explained elsewhere, the key to establishing freedom of movement is to separate *the natural right* of movement from various *positive law rights* such as citizenship, voting and public assistance.[148]

In summary, there are a number of policy changes that would immediately and substantially begin to reduce violence. End the foreign wars of intervention and bring the troops home. End the war on drugs. The drug war fuels crime and even terrorism in dozens of countries around the world and in all of America's cities. Cut the United States Military budget in half at least. That would improve the United States rank on the Human Freedom Index, would reduce United States foreign intervention

---

[147] Ludwig von Mises, *Liberalism: In the Classic Tradition* (1927).

[148] James Ostrowski, *A Libertarian Solution to the Immigration Crisis* Kindle Edition (2023).

which has been a disaster for decades,[149] and would also reduce the threat of terrorism that is often a response to foreign intervention.

With the end of the gun control movement, we can stop digging a deeper hole of ever-increasing government violence and start climbing out of that dark hole towards the light of liberty.

Table No. 9

A BOLD PLAN TO REDUCE
GLOBAL VIOLENCE

CATEGORY OF VIOLENCE	PROPOSALS TO MOVE TOWARD PEACE
GOVERNMENT VIOLENCE	END THE UNITED STATES GLOBAL MILITARY EMPIRE
	BRING THE TROOPS HOME
	ABOLISH THE WELFARE/TRANSFER PAYMENT STATE
	ABOLISH GOVERNMENT SCHOOLS
	ALLOW A FREE MARKET IN HEALTH CARE
CRIME	ENACT CONSTITUTIONAL CARRY
	END THE DRUG WAR

---

[149] See, Michael Ostrowski and James Ostrowski, *The Impeachment of Barack Obama and Hillary Clinton: for High Crimes in Syria and Libya* (2016).

CATEGORY OF VIOLENCE	PROPOSALS TO MOVE TOWARD PEACE
CRIME	ABOLISH GOVERNMENT SCHOOLS
	ABOLISH THE WELFARE STATE
WAR	NON-INTERVENTION INTO OTHER COUNTRIES
	FREE TRADE
	FLEXIBILITY AS TO BORDERS BASED ON PLEBISCITE AND LOCAL CONTROL
DEMOCIDE AND TERRORISM	GLOBAL RIGHT TO BEAR ARMS
	FLEXIBILITY AS TO BORDERS BASED ON PLEBISCITE
	RECOGNIZE A NATURAL RIGHT TO PEACEFUL FREE MOVEMENT (EXCLUDING CITIZENSHIP, VOTING AND WELFARE)

Conclusion

From time immemorial and currently, human beings without the means to protect themselves have been wrongly and unjustly beset upon by governments, states, kingdoms, fiefdoms, overlords, czars, politicians, generals, gendarmes, police, military, warlords, criminal gangs, crime syndicates, small groups of ruffians and lone thugs, and they have been beaten, shot, stabbed, burned, strangled, raped, robbed, extorted, enslaved, tortured, mutilated, kidnapped, imprisoned, detained, searched, interrogated, executed, driven from their homes, driven from their countries, exiled, prevented from leaving their homes, neighborhoods or nations without permission, conscripted, forced to be cannon fodder in pointless wars where they are killed, maimed or permanently traumatized; and they have had their money, wealth, possessions and homes stolen and seized.

Worse yet, while many of these atrocities were spontaneous tragedies that soon ended, or were random and rare or could be anticipated and possibly prevented, and if not, were at least unlikely to be repeated, all of the above atrocities and malefactions done by states, politicians, kingdoms and the like, are continuing or permanent in nature and thus cannot be escaped, except for perhaps by fleeing in the middle of the night to yet another state or government that may be slightly less oppressive. In other words, for all practical purposes, *the malefactions inflicted on the individual by governments amount to a life sentence of brutalization.*

Miraculously, a solution to mankind's worst and oldest recurring nightmare was proffered around 400 years ago:[150] a natural right to bear arms. In this revolutionary new approach, the individual human being at long last had a natural moral right to bear arms to defend himself against the government and the mob and the hoodlum. That natural right was recognized in positive law in 1791 in the Second Amendment and, as I proved in *The Second Amendment Works*, helped deter government tyranny against citizens and helped repel that rare foreign invasion during the War of 1812.

Now, in spite of the undeniable success of the right to bear arms in history and currently, there is an organized effort in the United States to destroy the right to bear arms and return individuals to that nightmarish state of helplessness in the face of criminals and tyrants they had suffered through for millennia and managed to escape only 233 years ago. The leaders of this sinister effort to destroy the most important human right are billionaires or government officials protected by a bevy of armed guards who live in safe, upscale neighborhoods protected by sophisticated security systems and transported in limousines.

The main weapon used by these gun controllers is deceit. They lie to the public constantly with a wide variety of dishonest or misleading statistics that are repeated endlessly by their lackeys in the media and in the schools.

These lies have been thoroughly exposed and refuted in this book and in the *Second Amendment Works* and they

---

[150] According to NGram, the term originated around 1582.

have been displaced by two new and powerful statistics that definitively prove the indispensable and efficacious nature of the right to bear arms.

Chapter Five presented for the first time a strategy to educate the public about the lies of the gun control movement and the truth about the right to bear arms.

We finally have a plan to defend, protect and *expand* the right to bear arms, *replace* the gun control movement with a *violence control movement,* and promote peace and liberty throughout the world. The rest is up to YOU!

Appendix

A Critique of the Global Peace Index

The Global Peace Index[151] (GPI), a well-funded and extremely sophisticated effort to rank countries by their degree of peacefulness, differs sharply from the conclusions reached in this book and thus merits a response. Specifically, it ranks the United States as the 132nd most peaceful country on Earth out of 163. In other words, the United States gets a poor grade from the GPI.

We do need a way to measure peace, however, I give the GPI a failing grade. For starters, they have no clear or coherent definition of peace or violence. In the peace business, that's a huge problem. How can you measure what you haven't defined? I have elsewhere defined peace as "the absence of violence or the palpable threat of violence against persons and their property."[152] An accurate measure of violence would begin with a proper definition of peace and would encompass and measure all forms of violence that transgress against peace. That is what I have done in this book.

The authors of the Global Peace Index give the violence committed on a daily basis by the modern state almost a complete pass. Indeed, they appear to *favor* a

---

[151] visionofhumanity.org

[152] J. Ostrowski, "The Myth of Democratic Peace: Why Democracy Cannot Deliver Peace in the 21st Century," mises.org (Feb. 19, 2005). https://www.lewrockwell.com/1970/01/james-ostrowski/the-myth-of-democratic-peace/

very strong state. As I have proven here, the state is the main source and cause of violence in this world both directly and indirectly.

Instead the GPI uses 23 "indicators" of violence, each of which is given equal weight in determining a country's overall score and ranking. Several of these are perfectly valid criteria. These include the number of homicides, prisoners, level of violent crime, terrorism and deaths from external conflict. Other criteria are problematical. The GPI gives positive weight to gun control efforts by measuring "ease of access to small arms and light weapons." However, I have already shown in this book that gun control is itself a form of violence against peaceful people. I have also shown in this book and in *The Second Amendment Works* that the right to bear arms deters many forms of violence including crime, state violence, war, civil war, democide and coups d'etat.

Several other criteria are subjective in nature and hence subject to bias or ideological influences on those scoring these factors. The major problem with the rating, however, is that it does not attempt to measure institutionalized state violence against citizens, which is, as I have concluded in this book, the single biggest factor in determining the level of violence in any society.

The Global Violence Index is based on measuring the five major forms of violence *directly* whereas the GPI uses several criteria that are subjective or which attempt to measure violence *indirectly*. It also includes improper criteria and excludes the major form of violence on the planet, government violence. For these reasons, I believe that my newly released Global Violence Index is a much more accurate ranking of countries based on their measurable quantities of violence and hence their departure from the ideal of peace.

Finally, because of these flaws in their methodology and because the GPI fails to address the actual sources and causes of violence in the world, it is not nearly as useful as the Global Violence Index in formulating and executing actual solutions to the major causes of violence in the world.

About the Author

James Ostrowski is a trial and appellate lawyer, author and podcaster from Buffalo, New York. He is the CEO of LibertyMovement.org, which promotes direct action strategies to achieve liberty.

He graduated from St. Joseph's Collegiate Institute in 1975 and obtained a degree in philosophy from the State University of New York at Buffalo in 1980. He graduated from Brooklyn Law School in 1983. In law school, he was writing assistant to Dean David G. Trager. He was a member of the Moot Court Honor Society and the International Law Moot Court Team. In 1984, he attended Professor Murray Rothbard's private seminar on the History of Economic Thought in New York City.

He served as vice-chairman of the law reform committee of the New York County Lawyers Association (1986-88) and wrote two widely quoted reports critical of the law enforcement approach to the drug problem. He was chair of the human rights committee, Erie County Bar Association (1997-1999) where he was an advocate for prisoners' rights. He has written a number of scholarly articles on the law on subjects ranging from drug policy to the commerce clause of the constitution to jury nullification.

His articles have appeared in the Wall Street Journal, Buffalo News, Cleveland Plain Dealer and Legislative Gazette. His policy studies have been published by the Hoover Institution, the Ludwig von Mises Institute, and the Cato Institute in Washington, D.C.

He is the author of *Government Schools Are Bad for Your Kids* (2009), *Direct Citizen Action* (2010), *Progressivism: A Primer* (2014) and *The Second Amendment Works* (2020).

He and his wife Amy live in North Buffalo and have two adult children. He was a long-time youth baseball and basketball coach. His hobbies include speed chess and hiking.